MW00908882

What The Hell Do We Do Now?

An enterprise guide to COVID-19 and beyond

By

Butler, Hagan, Hodgson et. al.

Kienco
PO Box 37
Deer Park Vic 3023, Australia

First Edition
First Published in 2020

Illustrations by Danny McKibben and Lynne Cazaly

Publisher's Cataloging-in-Publication data
Butler, M., Hagan, A., Hodgson, B., et. al.
What The Hell Do We Do Now?: An enterprise guide to COVID-19 and beyond / Butler, Hagan, Hodgson et.al.

ISBN 978-0-6489661-2-8 Paperback

1. BUS071000 Business & Economics / Leadership
2. BUS063000 Business & Economics / Strategic Planning
3. BUS103000 Business & Economics / Organizational Development

Dedicated in loving memory to
Mervyn Silver, John Manuel & Helen Butler

The editors would like to thank:

Cassie Moore, Bill Ramsay, and Bernie Hagan, for the time and care you've taken to get this book ready for publication.

Our wonderful contributors for sharing your insights with us for this project.

Michelle Stedman, a conversation with whom inspired the idea for this book.

To everyone writing policies, washing hands, wearing masks, running tests, performing medical procedures, delivering meals, keeping an eye on the vulnerable or just simply staying at home to keep us all safe - thank you for the difference you're making.

Two-thirds of the editors would also like to thank The Oxford Comma for being useful, clarifying, and Mary's worst nightmare.

Contents

How to read this book 8

Introduction

Journey 11

Act I: Containment 25

Illusion of the Perfect World 27

Chapter One

Imagine 29

Realisation 49

Chapter Two

Begin 51

Chapter Three

Design 65

Preparing for the Journey 81

Chapter Four

Purpose 83

Chapter Five

Shift 99

Act II: Transformation 115

The Descent 117

Chapter Six

Legacy 119

Chapter Seven

Support 137

The Eye of the Storm 151

Chapter Eight

Adapt 153

Chapter Nine

Perform 167

All is Lost 179

Chapter Ten

Plan 181

Chapter Eleven

Trust. 193

Act III: Emergence 209

Support 211

Chapter Twelve

Belong 213

Chapter Thirteen

Connect 227

The Moment of Truth. 245

Chapter Fourteen

Mindsafety 247

Chapter Fifteen

Tilt 259

Return to the Perfect World 271

Chapter Sixteen

Engage. 273

Chapter Seventeen

Sustain. 289

How to read this book

'What The Hell Do We Do Now' has been written with a practical focus - to help you to navigate the COVID-19 pandemic, and the real-world issues it's creating for leaders.

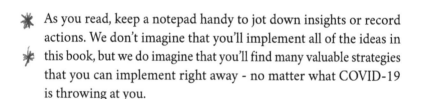

This book has been a collaboration between many world-class experts from diverse fields, with sometimes divergent points of view. Our role as curators has been to bring these experts' ideas together within a narrative framework that places you at the center as the heroine *(or hero)* of this journey of crisis, change, discovery, support and growth.

As you read, keep a notepad handy to jot down insights or record actions. We don't imagine that you'll implement all of the ideas in this book, but we do imagine that you'll find many valuable strategies that you can implement right away - no matter what COVID-19 is throwing at you.

We encourage you to use this book in the way you find it most helpful - either reading cover-to-cover OR using it as a reference for leading in the pandemic, dipping in-and-out of relevant chapters as the needs arise.

But most of all, we encourage you to bring others with you on this journey. To share the insights from the book with people in your team, your family, or your community.

After all, another way of saying *"we're all in this together"* is *"what elevates any of us elevates all of us"*.

Brent, Mary, and Alex

SCHMIDT'S HEROINE'S JOURNEY

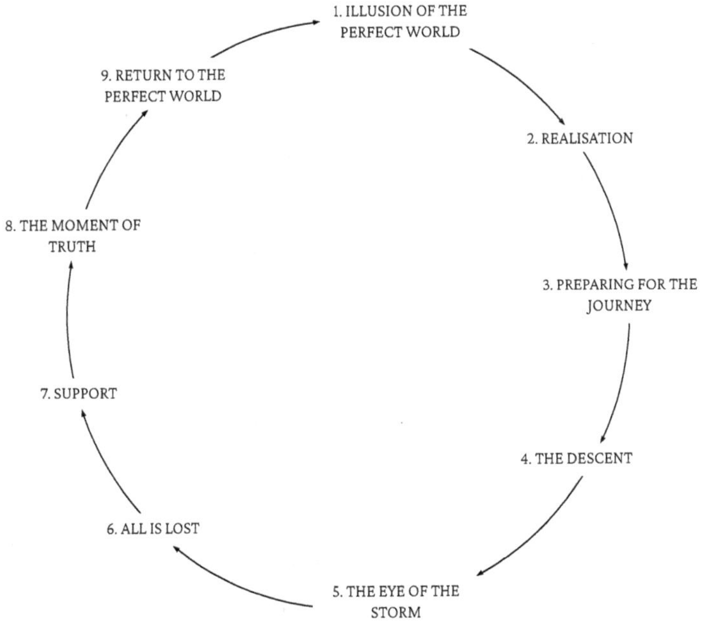

INTRODUCTION

Journey

Alex Hagan

For all the talk of 2020 Vision over the past few years, it turns out we had some pretty significant cataracts.

Here in Australia, the year started with one of the worst bushfire seasons on record. Dozens of people and up to a billion animals lost their lives, thousands of homes were destroyed, and communities were devastated. Before the first home was rebuilt, a global pandemic impacted the daily lives of almost every person on the planet. 7.8 billion people have had to confront their mortality and profoundly change their daily habits. We have had to make difficult decisions about our values and behaviours at a global scale.

This is not the 2020 Vision any of us had in mind.

Profound questions that run deep to the heart of who we are as a society have confronted us. We've had to decide how much a human life is worth in an environment where shutting down the economy means saving lives. We've grappled with what it means to make personal sacrifices for the common good. The COVID-19 pandemic and its ripple effects have accelerated trends in almost every industry. The implications will be long-term and possibly permanent. For the first time, we've made a clear distinction between social isolation and physical isolation, sweeping away the out-of-date distinction between online and 'in real life'. Trends in online education, health, commerce, and workforce have been dramatically brought forward. Many of us have learned what it means to wash our hands correctly for the first time and wondered why we didn't already know that. Maths education is sky-rocketing, at least as it relates to exponents, logarithmic graphs, and what it means to flatten them. The polite *"bless you"* has been replaced with the rather less courteous but much more effective *"get the f*&k away from me"*.

We are immigrants to the future. For years we've been talking about the potential of a Universal Basic Income to offset the effects of automation, a payment delivered to individuals without a work requirement or a means test. Critics and governments have wondered how it could possibly be funded. Yet, at least temporarily, something very similar to a wide-scale basic income of this type *(admittedly, not quite universal)* was adopted in Australia, with the doubling of JobSeeker payments and removal of the work test, and the introduction of JobKeeper for those who remain employed.

Employers who have historically insisted that work and the workplace are inextricably connected have severed that link out of necessity. In New Zealand, this first happened with just 48 hours notice, with no obvious disastrous consequences. Remote work, cited since the 1960s as *"The Future of Work"*, is now merely *"Work"*.

Education, too, has gone online for entire nations of children, and while this has been disruptive, it has also been productive, for the most part.

Telehealth has advanced years, as triage and treatment, where possible, has happened outside the traditional healthcare environments, and often from the driver's side window in the case of COVID-19 diagnosis. Telehealth is not a new concept, and is one that has been progressively enabled over time with increasing broadband penetration. The biggest issues have always been about regulation and funding, constrained by fear of fraud, service duplication, and quality issues. All of the sudden, the objections have melted away, and medicare funding rules were relaxed for telehealth appointments, allowing a boom in the sector.

Conferences and events have gone online, reducing financial, geographic, and social barriers to collaboration and learning. We did a pre-launch of our book at one of these - for the first time in its 14-year history, the Australiasian Talent Conference was held entirely online, and the result was a roster of global speakers and triple the usual number of delegates, from a range of countries not previously represented.

Communities have come together digitally while being distanced physically, with spontaneous acts of kindness, and teddy-bears in the windows to comfort and delight children at a time where comfort is needed.

International borders have closed, and trade barriers have been erected. Business leaders in Tijuana, Mexico called for that wall on the border - not to keep Mexicans from migrating to the USA, but to stop Americans bringing COVID-19 to Mexico. Julian Palombo, a Tijuana business chamber, was cited by Reuters as saying. *"It makes sense to build a wall, but a public health wall from over there to here to avoid the risk of possible infections."*[1]

We have stretched the present into the future, and it's still unclear whether the world will snap back to its previous dimensions. We get to choose.

Perhaps the link between knowledge work and its location has been permanently severed - employers now know that they can hire the best talent in the world, not just the best talent within commuting distance from their offices, and occasionally let them work from home. Education could become increasingly virtualised on a more permanent basis. The shift would give society many opportunities, such as having the people who wrote the textbook teach the lessons. Geography, class sizes, and wealth do not need to determine access to education and subject choice. The School of the Air has been teaching children in remote communities since 1951, five years before the first TV signal was broadcast in Australia, but it took 7 decades before we tried it wholesale. We may have had a permanent re-shaping of community values, geopolitical relationships, and our desire and ability to travel around the world. In all sorts of ways, the world has changed irrevocably.

---

1 Diaz, L., 2020. Mexicans wonder if Trump's wall could stop coronavirus spreading south. Reuters, [online] Available at: <https://www.reuters.com/article/us-health-coronavirus-mexico-wall/mexicans-wonder-if-trumps-wall-could-stop-coronavirus-spreading-south-idUSKBN21003G>.

There is no clear path back to normal - when you're in unchartered territory, all maps are useless.

Yet, for all our desire for a return to normality, there was a creeping awareness before the pandemic that perhaps normal wasn't all that desirable in the first place. Global threats such as climate change have never been far from the front of mind for decades, yet they have often been met with responses ranging from disbelief, to indifference, to inaction by many. Inequality is rising in the developed world. Popularist, demigogue political leaders are becoming ever more common, and xenophobia and nationalism are on the rise as a frightened public seek simplistic solutions to a complex and frenetic world in which they are feeling left behind.

Economic growth has been one of the greatest gifts to our society. In just the last 170 years, advanced economies have experienced a phenomenal gain in both life expectancy and quality of life. In just the past four decades, billions have been lifted out of poverty in what we once referred to as the second and third worlds. But the growth cannot be sustained forever. Our runaway capitalist society has led to increasing demand for production, far beyond the point of social and ecological sustainability.

Despite the tragic human cost, the events of 2020 have demonstrated that when it comes down to it, we value people over profit.

As a threat subsides, we have an opportunity to pause and reset. We can leave behind these practices that no longer serve us. We can have a more sustainable, collegiate, and caring world, and we can realise that our economy is only a part of that world, and not the most important part at that.

In the early days of the pandemic, many were referring to the event as a Black Swan, a term popularized by Nassim Nicholas Taleb in his 2007 book of the same name[2]. A Black Swan event is one that is impossible to predict, and explainable only in retrospect. Rather, COVID-19 is better described as a Grey Rhino[3]. Black Swan Events and Grey Rhino Events have key commonalities - they are rare, they are high impact, and they are neglected until they have arrived. What differs between the two, however, is critical - black swans are often not predictable, but are explainable only in retrospect. Grey Rhinos, on the other hand, occur only after a series of warnings and visible evidence of their likelihood. Grey rhinos got their name for two reasons - firstly, while all rhinos are grey, the two most commonly known species are called *"black rhinos"* and *"white rhinos"*. Despite clearly visible evidence, we always misclassify rhinos and don't acknowledge them for what they are. The second reason is that when a two-ton grey rhino is coming towards you, it's a good idea to prepare for impact, or get out of the way.

This rhino, and others like it, have been coming our way for some time. The Johns Hopkins University, in collaboration with the World Economic Forum, ran a pandemic preparation simulation as late as 15 October of last year, merely 33 days before the first known case of COVID-19. It was the fourth time the institution had run such a simulation over 18 years, and the summary of key findings was the same as it had been on all three previous occasions: *"We are nowhere near prepared."*[4]. Pandemics have routinely made the list of the most significant global risks in the World Economic Forum's annual

---

2 Taleb, N., 2010. The Black Swan: The Impact Of The Highly Improbable. 2nd ed. Prince Frederick, MD: Recorded Books.

3 A term coined by Michelle Wucker in her 2016 book. Wucker, M., 2016. The Gray Rhino: How To Recognise And Act On The Obvious Dangers We Ignore. 1st ed. New York: St Martin's Press.

4 Pearce, K., 2019. Pandemic simulation exercise spotlights massive preparedness gap. Johns Hopkins University Hub, [online] Available at: <https://hub.jhu.edu/2019/11/06/event-201-health-security/>.

Global Risks Report, ranking fourth in potential impact in 2007[5], and 5th in 2008[6]. Bill Gates was warning of the next pandemic in a TED Talk in 2015. Even one of my favourite childhood books, a choose-your-own-adventure-style novel called *Freeway Fighter,* published in 1985, was set in a post-pandemic 2022.

SARS, MERS, and even the common cold are all forms of coronavirus for which there is no commercially available vaccine[7]; there is no vaccine for HIV or Ebola, despite significant efforts to find one. Pandemics are, in fact, a recurring event around the world, and we are at the mercy of fate as to the combination of the R0 *("R nought")* score *(contagion)* and the case fatality rate as to the impact that they will have. At the time of writing, it looks like COVID-19 has an R0 of around 5.7, meaning that the average person infected with the virus infects 5.7 others when uncontained by social distancing, masks, and the other precautions we've become increasingly accustomed to. This is three times more contagious than the 1918 flu pandemic, and 4 times more contagious than the H1N1 flu in 2009. For those who are infected with COVID-19, the case fatality rate is relatively low at 2.65%, as compared to, say, Ebola, with a case fatality rate of 50%, but far greater than the seasonal flu with a case fatality rate of less than 0.1%.

---

5 World Economic Forum, Citigroup, Marsh & McLennon Companies (MMC), Swiss Re, Wharton School Risk Center. 2007. Global Risks 2007: A Global Risk Network Report. [online] Geneva: World Economic Forum. Available at: <http://www3.weforum.org/docs/WEF_Global_Risks_Report_2007.pdf>.

6 World Economic Forum, Citigroup, Marsh & McLennon Companies (MMC), Swiss Re, Wharton School Risk Center, Zurich Financial Services. 2008. Global Risks 2008: A Global Risk Network Report. [online] Geneva: World Economic Forum. Available at: <http://www3.weforum.org/docs/WEF_Global_Risks_Report_2007.pdf>.

7 Though, in the case of MERS the virus went away before a viable vaccine candidate went through stage 3 trials.

Early in the pandemic, many people were claiming that COVID-19 was a storm in a teacup because the flu killed more people each year. That is no longer true, and is testament the limits of our obsession with data and where it can lead us astray. When the world changes or we have a novel, disruptive factor like a never-before seen pandemic, relying on past data is unhelpful - and especially so in exponential times. By definition, we don't have last year's data about something that didn't exist last year. All the data we have is about the past. All the decisions we make are about the future. Delays in understanding the exponential growth of the virus have been catastrophic in those countries that were slow to respond.

The Justinian plague, commonly known as the Black Death, was active in London for more than 300 years. Whilst we speak of a first, second, and third wave for the coronavirus, London experienced more than 40 waves of the black plague over 300 years, each one killing approximately 20% of its population. There is no guarantee, but a good chance, that a viable vaccine for COVID-19 can be found, produced at scale, and be accessed globally. Even if it is, then there is no going back to a pre-2020s sense of normal. The world will have changed, whether we consciously shape that evolution or not. We've already seen that the crisis has created an opportunity to accelerate trends, to innovate, and to build community. My hope is that our selves, our organisations, our societies, our economies, and our planet emerge from this unfamiliar territory in a better condition than we entered it. The path forward is clouded, but the future will be shaped by the choices we make now nonetheless.

We're culturally attuned to stories where the heroes are seeking treasure, slaying dragons, or rescuing princesses. The hero makes an active choice to go on these adventures. These types of chest-beating masculine heroic archetypes echo through films like Star Wars, video games like Super Mario Brothers, and some of the most epic stories throughout history - as shown in Joseph Campbell's book *"The Hero with a Thousand Faces"*.[8]

That's not the kind of hero we need right now. We didn't seek out this unfamiliar world, it was thrust upon us. The enemy is invisible, we'll defeat it together, and we won't get any medals for doing it. The battle won't be won with the use of armies, lightsabers, or even magic mushrooms. Wearing a mask, sheltering in place, keeping a respectful physical distance, practicing effective personal hygiene, connecting with and protecting loved ones, researching innovations, and making sure nobody's needs go unmet - these are hardly the plot lines of the next blockbuster Hollywood action flick, but they're exactly what we need at a time when our best chance of building a better future is to work together for common good.

We're embarking on a new hero's journey. One that is perhaps less like Campbell's masculine chest-beating dragon-slaying archetype, and more like Victoria Lynn Schmidt's Heroine's Journey[9]. Not an external journey to slay a dragon, but an internal one to find what we truly value, and rise to the challenge of being the leaders our communities need.

As you read this book, you'll be taken on your own journey - through the three acts, and nine stages of Schmidt's Heroine's Journey. In each chapter of this journey, our hand-picked co-authors will share their perspectives and insights on what is needed to journey through the crisis and emerge stronger as organisations, and perhaps also as people.

---

8 Campbell, J., 1956. The Hero With A Thousand Faces. Meridian Books.

9 Schmidt, V., 2007. 45 Master Characters: Mythic Models for Creating Original Characters. Cincinatti: Writer's Digest Books.

The hero at the centre of this journey is you.

Summary:

The future is impossible to predict, but possible to influence.

COVID-19 has challenged us to confront our values and enabled innovations long-thought to be impractical, often in a very short timeframe.

We will not be going back to a pre-2020 type of 'normal', whether we want to or not. What comes next depends on the choices we make and the actions we take today.

Questions:

1. When you think about the trends that are driving the future of your organisation, industry, or life, what comes to mind?
2. What are the grey rhinos in your organisation - the things that you know will have a high impact and are likely to happen, but that you don't have a plan for yet?
3. What are the choices and actions you can take today to step towards your preferred future, and mitigate the greatest risks you see?
4. If you were starting your organisation today, with the same vision statement, how would you do things differently?
5. If crisis is a reset button, what can you do today to set the conditions for your future success?

About the Author:

Alex Hagan

Alex Hagan is a futurist who helps organisations face fundamentally unpredictable futures with confidence, and is the author of *"Thriving in Complexity: The Art and Science of discovering opportunity in the New Normal" (2019)*. With a background spanning Econometrics, Workforce Strategy, Software Product Management and Applied Foresight, Alex has worked with governments, corporations, and communities on every populated continent to explore, imagine, and create the future of their industries, organisations, and workforces.

From a break room in Boronia to the ballroom of the Washington Convention Centre, Alex is a globally sought after speaker, facilitator and advisor, and equips people the tools they need to create a future that takes advantage of the unprecedented complexity in the way we live and work today. Alex is the founder and CEO of boutique Strategic Workforce Planning consultancy, Kienco.

Act I: Containment

Illusion of the Perfect World

in which the hero is in a safe world of things known to her and has a false sense of security about her future

CHAPTER ONE

Imagine

Dr Richard Hodge

Imagine the world was a snow dome. Imagine some giant shaking it, watching the disruption falling over land, under water and amid the air. He knows the outer coating is wafer thin, a finely balanced gaseous case. Yet still he shakes it, distributing pollution, raising the temperature, and watching its living contents scurrying and succumbing to disruption as microdots of plastic fill the ecosystem.

Imagine watching the little people. So many of them, battling for survival. Strange little people, hunting and gathering what they need from the Earth. Some herding animals and growing plants. Social little people. Gathering in communities. Lots of communities of their own making. Innovative little people. Some building homes, roads, bridges and networks of all kinds connecting people. Some singing songs. Some drilling holes in search of an oozing, black pus they burn in different ways. Black energy. In so many devices. Divisive little people, warring and fighting, suppressing and oppressing. Thoughtful little people. Depressed little people. Scared little people slowly awakening to a giant killing the world that gives them life.

Imagine the giant cared. Would he stop shaking the globe so viscerally?

Imagine the giant. His name is Greed. Human Greed. A satirical presence giving form to the question of whether humans are inherently corrupt or whether they become corrupted? Imagine the latter.

We don't have to imagine greed and corruption. We lived through a global financial crisis. We largely ignored the loss of ethics at its core. Finance is an easy fix. Ethics, not so. For that goes to mindset and behaviour and changing what we have become. Addicted to power, position and privilege we failed to address the global ethics crisis. We were engaged in the system sufficient to ignore the root cause of corruption of the system. We nodded politely to the triple bottom line of planet, people and profit and buried two of them in obscurity. Cash is king.

Eight years later, multiple testimonies to Australia's Royal Commission into Banking, Superannuation and Financial Services brought evidence of the deep personal and social consequences of institutions putting profit before people. The Aged Care Royal Commission added to the unmasking of economic greed, and loss of ethics, finding profiteers working to *"bleed them dry until they die .*[1]*"* Is this our future?

---

1 See ABC Four Corners Program, aired 26 June 2017, Available online https://www.abc.net.au/4corners/bleeding-them-dry-promo/8643348

When economics is in the driver's seat, human greed and corruption ride shotgun in the shadows. With each review, we create a chance to make a different world. Yet, when the Royal Commission into Banking, Superannuation and Financial Services says remuneration of executives tells people what the organisation values [2], it institutionalises personal drive for positions of *"value"* over social consequence, keeping open the door to corruption. It feeds the giant to a point where eight people have more wealth combined than *"the poorest half of the human race.* [3]*"* Too few stop to consider the ethics of such inequity.

The market charts the rise and fall of stocks, the corporate heartbeat. Growth is the goal and people optimise for efficiency to eke out another percentage point of productivity. Efficiency drives higher profits yet increases the fragility of our enterprises and the social and ecological fabric. Efficiency squeezes the economy in ways that fractures the foundations on which our economy stands *(Figure 1).*

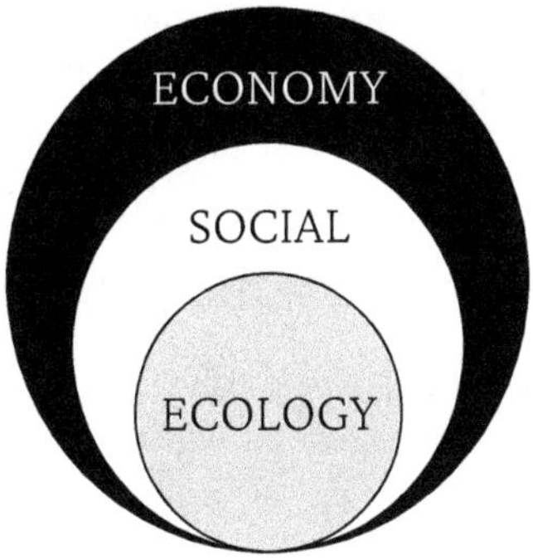

Figure 1: Economy first, Planet last, Social squeezed

2 See Final Report: https://www.royalcommission.gov.au/sites/default/files/2019-02/fsrc-volume-1-final-report.pdf

3 Oxfam (2017) "An Economy for the 99%" https://www.oxfam.org.au/wp-content/uploads/2017/07/oxfam-An-economy-for-the-99-percent-oz-factsheet.pdf

The World Wildlife Fund's *(WWF)* Living Planet Report shows population sizes of wildlife decreased by 60% globally between 1970 and 2014. It reported the *"Exploding human consumption is the driving force behind the unprecedented planetary change we are witnessing, through the increased demand for energy, land and water... The products we consume, the supply chains behind them, the materials they use and how these are extracted and manufactured have myriad impacts on the world around us.* [4]*"*

Mike Barrett, [then] executive director of science and conservation at WWF, said *"We are sleepwalking towards the edge of a cliff ... If there was a 60% decline in the human population, that would be equivalent to emptying North America, South America, Africa, Europe, China and Oceania. That is the scale of what we have done.* [5]*"*

Technology will not fix this. *"Advancing technology allows us to skate closer to the cliff than ever before.* [6]*"* The answer lies in nature. *"Protecting biodiversity is as important as fighting climate change,"* said Robert Watson, chair of the Intergovernmental Panel on Biodiversity and Ecosystem Services *(IPBES)* speaking in Medellin, Colombia on 22 March 2018[7]. The destruction of nature is as dangerous as climate change. And, it continues unabated.

---

4 "Living Planet Report" World Wildlife Fund. Available online (last accessed, 22 May 2020) https://www.wwf.org.uk/sites/default/files/2018-10/wwfintl_livingplanet_full.pdf

5 Damian Carrington, "The age of extinction" Environment editor, The Guardian. 30 October 2018 See: https://www.theguardian.com/environment/2018/oct/30/humanity-wiped-out-animals-since-1970-major-report-finds

6 Rick Dove (2019) Systems Engineering Society of Australia Workshop, October 2019 (and author, Response Ability: The Language, Structure and Culture of the Agile Enterprise, Wiley, 2001)

7 Reported by Jonathan Watts, The Guardian, https://www.theguardian.com/environment/2018/mar/23/destruction-of-nature-as-dangerous-as-climate-

Imagine it different.

Nicholas Nassim Taleb, author of The Black Swan and Antifragile – Things that Gain from Disorder, was asked[8] what he learnt from Daniel Kahneman, Nobel Laureate on behavioural economics. His short answer was, *"I learned one can force people to have a healthy outlook."* This doesn't mean calling out the National Guard. In his longer answer he said,

> *"The first idea that [Kahneman] gave me is that people do not perceive stand-alone objects, rather differences away from an anchor point. He said that it was not cultural: even the vision of babies was based on identifying variations. It was simply more economical for the brain to do so ... They just take a benchmark and react to variations from it. So, one could make them react more rationally by modifying the anchor."*

Imagine what we can do if we change an anchor. We change something in a person's context that consequently leads them *"to have a realistic outlook on things." (Taleb, 2014)*

Imagine a new anchor

One idea I took from Prashant Dhawan[9], CEO Biomimicry India, is the profound idea to prioritise ecology – for all life, not just human

---

change-scientists-warn, 24 March 2018

8 "Daniel Kahneman changed the way we think about thinking. But what do other thinkers think of him?" The Observer, 16 February 2014, Available online https://www.theguardian.com/science/2014/feb/16/daniel-kahneman-thinking-fast-and-slow-tributes (Last accessed, 3 Jun 2020)

9 Prashant Dhawan "Biomimicry" – Keynote presentation to the International Symposium of the International Council on Systems Engineering, Orlando, FL. USA, 20-25 July 2019

life – to live in a natural world containing a complex mix of societies each with their own economic view. Each context nests within, and serves, the other without being corrupted by the squeeze of economic gain. Good economics results from a vibrant society results from a healthy ecology. This visionary difference is shown in Figure 2. Ecology of the planet comes first. It's the one home for all the living things we know. The revised nesting of these three views offers a new anchor. Whereas an economic anchor is premised on growth, an ecological anchor is premised on strict limits to growth, as the planetary resources are finite. The new anchor comes with a single condition for all decision making – first do no harm.

Imagine all our decisions made with a new anchor – ecology-led not economy-led.

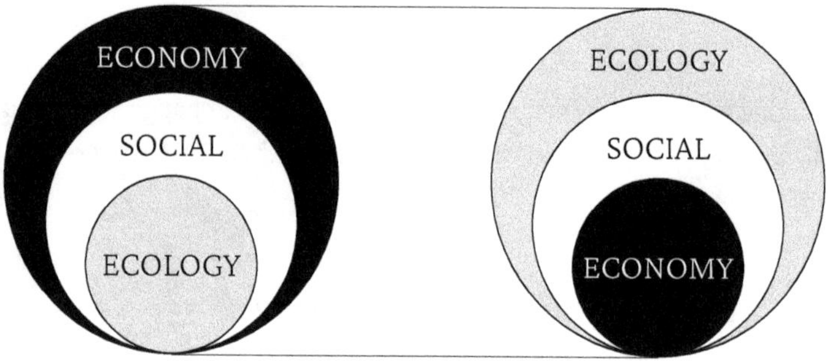

Figure 2: Change the Anchor to Assure the Survival of All Life

Imagine talking with your grandchildren of the days when the black, oil-rich economy governed our lives. How we felt the squeeze of goals, targets, earnings, profit, position, power, and privilege. How profit came before people. How people scoured the planet for profit. Constantly spinning in a vicious cycle of growth and greed, possession and dispossession, life and death.

Imagine today is the past and our ecological future becomes our children's reality

> *"You may live in the world as it is, but you can still work to create the world as it should be." - Michelle Obama*

We have no other choice. We can only work from where we are, towards leaving a better legacy than if we do nothing. Let us imagine applying Taleb's lesson he took from Kahneman. Let's imagine creating a better world, by changing the anchor we use today.

Imagine Our Journey to a Better Future

The Stockdale Paradox – made famous by Jim Collins – was a feature of all 'good-to-great companies. *"You must maintain unwavering faith that you can and will prevail in the end, regardless of the difficulties, AND at the same time have the discipline to confront the most brutal facts of your current reality, whatever they might be.* [10]*"*

Let's hold faith in the future of the planet and the new anchor we give a damn about. The arrival of COVID-19 changed everyone's anchor. For most, survival mattered more than money. Behaviour changed. Pollution lessened. People in Delhi, India saw the Himalayas for the first time in 30 years. People cared. Some governments cared for the social fabric and the health of their people ahead of the economy. Opening the original 'first wave' restrictions with care, Victorian Premier Dan Andrews stated that he wanted to do it *"... taking slow, cautious, steady, graduated and safe steps so that we do this once and do it properly* [11]*."* Trust in governments, so low before the pandemic,

10 Jim Collins (2001) Good to Great, Harper Collins, New York p.13

11 The Age online edition, 24 May 2020, https://www.theage.com.au/national/victoria/victoria-moves-to-dramatically-ease-coronavirus-restrictions-

is tentatively being revived. Political sniping is at an all-time low. There's reason to hope a better future is achievable.

Could there be better timing than now to build on this shift?

Imagine Taking Action

Let's also face up. The harsh reality is still here. We feel angst before acting and have to address our internal conflicts. Look in the mirror.

If we don't do it already, it behoves all of us to look in the mirror, and consider three questions:

1. What do I care about – actually give a damn about – for the planet, people and our economy?

The answer to this question paints a picture of our personal anchors in life. The strength of our attachment drives our individual actions. If our lives are not serving the people and matters we give a damn about why are we here? Where else will we ever find purpose and identity?

2. In what ways does my organisation give a damn about the planet, the people and economy?

The answer to this question paints a picture of the business / organisational context we find ourselves in. It's good to know where others stand if we are standing and working with them.

20200524-p54vvo.html

The emergence of this line of thinking enables each of us to identify any gaps and describe them without value judgement. We accept it's just different.

(The same question can be addressed for our family, community groups, national and international groups we're a part of.)

3. What, if anything, am I going to do about that difference, knowing silence condones the difference?

The answer to this question sets an agenda for action. It opens an internal dialogue about vulnerability. Am I prepared to state openly what I give a damn about? And, listen to what others might say in complete contravention of everything I hold dear?

I believe too many of us fear letting go of the old anchors, not because we don't give a damn about our new anchors, but we allow the vulnerability and fear of exposure to hold us back from action. All the while our yearning for change feeds a war within.

> “*If you avoid conflict to keep the peace, you start a war inside yourself*" - *Cheryl Richardson*

There's conflict either way – inside us when we hold on to old anchors, or outside us as we try to change anchors with others who give a damn about different things or about the same things, differently. Progress depends on small groups working well together for a better future[12].

---

12 As often quoted from Margaret Mead, "Never doubt that a small group of thoughtful, committed citizens can change the world; indeed, it's the only thing

So, which conflict are you living with, right now – the war inside you, or the conflict with others? Imagine the only conflicts you face are the ones arising from you acting on the things you actually give a damn about. Aren't those the battles worth fighting?

Imagine the difference you will make

Look out the window. Externally, the harsh reality of death and economic loss of COVID have been of such magnitude to silence media interest in climate change, at least for the moment.

Despite these losses, or perhaps because of them, we can draw some comfort because our COVID reality is shared by billions of humans. Among them, millions of people who – like us – actually give a damn about the state of the planet as much as we do and want our corporations to play their part in fixing it, not just destroying it.

People who actually give a damn about living in a society not an economy and want our corporations to put people before profit *(hint: it builds brand and loyalty).*

People who give a damn about all life, not just human life. The natural order is systemic. We want our corporations to think and act systemically in harmony with nature.

Look through the management window. The harsh reality we face in our economy is the mantra *"if you can't measure it, you can't manage it."* It's a myth. The systemic nature of the world, the interconnectedness

---

that ever has."

of our complex adaptive enterprises means our understanding of reality is at best partial, tentative and subjective[13].

Despite this, the myth lurks in daily practice as managers trained in reductionist thinking are seduced by numbers. They hope to find clarity and security in the apparent objectivity numbers and charts provide. They cascade these into the organisation digging deep into the souls of people struggling to achieve a target at any cost.

Imagine changing the measures

Measurement systems are hard to bust open and change. Yet, when people die, we don't find it so hard. Obituaries don't start or finish with economics, nor even mention economic performance. Tom Peters observed[14] at age 71 that he's now been to a lot of funerals and he's not seen one gravestone mention the nett worth of an individual.

In celebrating a life, we count the value of who the person was being, the contribution they gave and the difference they made to others and the planet. We laud a person generous with their time, attention and money. A person who did their best in their context. We measure their value not by numbers over time, not by beginnings and endings, but by how they influenced the ongoing story of their social setting while they were present.

Imagine those measures being our stock-in-trade

---

13 Geert Hofstede (1996). The Influence of Nationality on Organization Theories Organization Studies, 1996, Vol. 17 No.3: 525-537

14 "Tom Peters on Leading in the 21st Century" McKinsey Quarterly, September 2014

Our challenge is not to wait till death to start counting the value of a contribution in this way. A new anchor warrants new measures and a new way of measuring. What difference have we made to the things we really give a damn about? My hope is for you to begin asking this question. Value and relevance. That's all we need. Let it start when you next look in the mirror.

Imagine overcoming the vulnerability you might feel.

Imagine framing your next report to the market with kindness as an obituary on the last counting period.

Imagine projecting through your leadership window the sense of well-being and affirmation over contributions made, not targets missed.

Imagine numbers prevailing. For some will not change quickly. The competitive eyes of the market will be prying for weakness, for reason to sell your stock, with vultures circling to raid your business.

What leaders count, counts. If we only feed them numbers, they will feed only on our numbers.

Imagine economic numbers never again standing alone

The idea of a Triple Bottom Line has been with us for over 50 years. It was born in the old order, anchored in economics. Analysts and their critics have been exploring ways to bring ecological and social matters to an economic figure – a nett present value of sorts conceived as human capital *(how labour is used to derive economic value)* and eco-capitalism *(which uses market-based policy instruments to resolve environmental problems).* Everything brought to economic account in the old anchor.

Imagine instead a Triple Bottom Line exists in the new order, anchored in ecology where growth requires a continuous supply of energy. What then, if energy units were a base measure as well as dollars? What if we knew the energy cost of every dollar in circulation? What if we knew the carbon dioxide emission for every dollar? When we extract more energy resources from the Earth than we gain free from the Sun, the planet is in energy deficit. When we emit more carbon dioxide than naturally occurs in the air, we invoke a planetary deficit. A family or a corporation would be able to make a crude assessment of their contribution to the energy and carbon dioxide deficits.

We know that the average human needs 2,000 food calories a day to stay alive, which is about 100W of energy – akin to running a light bulb. We also know that the average per capita consumption of energy is 3,000W per day, with a peak of 11,000W in the United States. We have built societies that place constant pressure of an overwhelming energy deficit on the planet.

Yet today, in Australia, we worry more about the economic recession coming from our response to COVID-19. It will be the first recession in 29 years and the forecast is that worse is yet to come. There is now *"no chance"* of avoiding a deep recession but *"we can work to ensure the recession is as shallow and short as possible.* [15]*"* It's seen as a crisis.

---

15 Patrick Durkin "Australia Dangerously Exposed to a Deep Recession" Article in Australian Financial Review, 21 May 2020, https://www.afr.com/policy/economy/australia-most-exposed-to-great-crash-20200521-p54v1u

We might worry about the first economic recession in three decades yet we have failed to take action on the harsh reality that the planet has been in an energy recession for over 200 years. If the ecology were the economy, we would have taken action 199 years ago.

We've been seduced by the mantra, *"it's the economy, stupid."* Yet, by changing to an ecological anchor, let us change mantras with full faith, *"it's all energy, stupid.* [16]"

Imagine if governments that give a damn about the ecology of the planet responded as quickly to planetary recession as they do to an economic one. It's not yet too late.

Imagine corporations that give a damn not waiting for regulation to force their hand. They need energy to grow. It's how they source it that matters. Imagine shareholders who give a damn asking their Boards to make their new triple bottom line transparent.

Imagine the transformation illustrated in Figure 3 when we put the planet and people ahead of profit.

---

16 Geoffrey West, Scale – The Universal Laws of Growth, Innovation, Sustainability and the Pace of Life in Organisms, Cities, Economies and Companies Penguin Press, New York, 2017

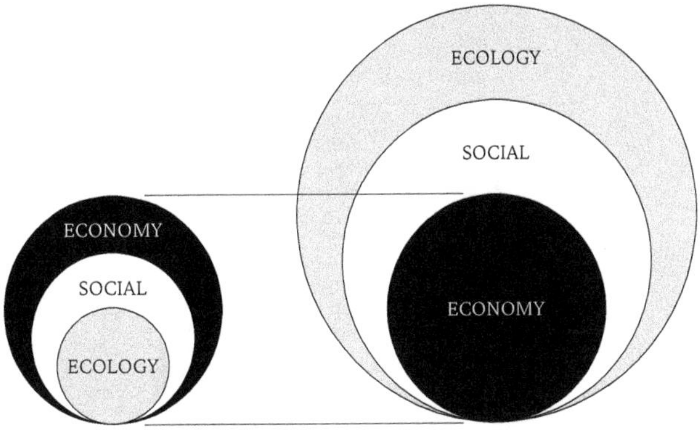

Figure 3: Economic growth depends on ecological and social growth

Maybe then we will see today's economic attention shift to a full balance sheet of planetary and social costs. Imagine that energy flowing to social and ecological issues on which the economy depends. Everything survives and grows from the flow of energy, not just the economy.

Maybe then the giant will handle the snow globe with care. Holding it up to the sunshine that gives it life. Watching the Earth slowly repair and grow. The scars of the old anchor will be visible as they must. For we must carry those stories through our children and grandchildren so they never repeat the mistakes of the past.

Imagine the giant returning the globe to ecological growth counted by increasing diversity in habitat and species. Imagine the new growth of social equality and respect because we gave a damn about the true provenance of how we grow our economies.

Imagine the future. It's right here.

It's ours if we give a damn enough to demand it.

Summary:

COVID has momentarily changed our economic anchor, creating time and space for us to care about people and planet before profit.

The harsh reality is the planet has been in an energy recession for over 200 years, which has killed 60% of all animal population since 1970. If it were an economic recession, we'd have acted 199 years ago.

We can lead people to change how they think and act if we change our anchor from an economic focus to an ecological focus requiring systemic thinking and action in every dimension. It's more demanding, but it's natural.

Questions:

1. To what extent can you clearly state what you care about – actually give a damn about – for the planet, people and our economy?
2. What is the likelihood, you will raise your voice to be heard on the issues you give a damn about?
3. To what extent do your organisation's senior executives give a damn about the planet, the people *(especially outside the organisation)* and the economy?
4. How strongly do you feel about doing something to address the difference between your convictions and your organisation's activities?
5. To what extent are you ready to change? How will you feel if you do nothing with the opportunity you have to shape the future?

About the Author:

Dr. Richard Hodge

Richard obsesses about wholeness, knowing everything is connected to this pale blue dot of a planet in an insignificant galaxy. That perspective drives him to work with millennials and planetary leaders to build the capability they need in systemic intervention. He does this through speaking, coaching and mentoring programs. His background in systems science, systems engineering, strategy, governance and large-scale transformation spans a range of industries in public and private enterprise. He brings complex ideas to life with a practical focus to enable leaders – especially emerging leaders – take a 'first do no harm' approach for our planet and the people who call it home.

Realisation

in which the hero is pushed to a fork in the road where she must make a choice between facing her fears or staying where she is

CHAPTER TWO

Begin

Dr Monique Beedles

Antediluvian is a beautiful word that literally means before the flood. It references the Biblical flood of Noah and is used tongue in cheek to refer to something that's ridiculously old-fashioned, like when your teenage child tells you that your clothes are positively antediluvian. I live in Brisbane, Australia, a sub-tropical city built on a flood plain and in 2011, a 100-year flood decimated our city. Everyone who lives here can bookmark their lives by this flood, before and after. What we learned in 2011 is that before the flood could actually be very recent[1]. The silt is still drying, that musty and slightly sickening smell still hangs in the air. It's not long ago, but it's a shift so significant that it can define a lifetime. While antediluvian literally means before the flood, it really means *before everything changed.*

---

1 Beedles, M., 2011. Pivot Point: making the decisions that matter in business. Brisbane: Teak Yew Pty Ltd.

The Brewing Storm

In the 1990s, during the midst of a biotech boom, I conducted my doctoral research on the strategic imperatives in the global pharmaceutical industry[2]. The most important assets of a pharmaceutical company are its patents[3]. These patents have a finite lifecycle, expiring at twenty years. It can take fifteen years, and billions of dollars, from the time a patent is first registered to when it finally becomes a marketable product. That leaves only a small window for companies to make back their money before others make a generic copy. This was an industry with a clear imperative to innovate. Now, every industry has an imperative to innovate.

For the past decade, we have lived in the aftermath of the Global Financial Crisis. Capital has been constrained across the globe, banks have faced liquidity challenges, and governments have intervened with major capital and infrastructure investments in an attempt to stabilise markets and their own currencies[4]. In an era of low interest rates, capital growth is not guaranteed and negative growth is commonplace. Value can no longer be reliably created merely by owning capital assets[5].

---

2 Beedles, M., 2002. The uncertain role of alliances in the strategic armoury of the dominant firms in the global pharmaceutical industry. Brisbane: QUT PhD Thesis.

3 Beedles, M., 2016. Asset Management for Directors. Sydney: Australian Institute of Company Directors.

4 Milchevaa, S., Falkenbachb, H. & Markmannc, H., 2019. Bank liquidity management through the issuance of bonds in the aftermath of the global financial crisis. Research in International Business and Finance, Volume 48, pp. 32-47.

5 Beedles, M., 2019. The imperative for innovation in asset management. Fremantle, Asset Management Council.

Late in 2007, Australia ratified the Kyoto Protocol, signalling a global shift in the way we address environmental imperatives. The challenge to preserve our natural world in concert with human flourishing requires innovation. We need to achieve sustainable outcomes by making better use of existing resources and doing more with less. In parallel with this, the relative importance of tangible and intangible assets has shifted dramatically over the last 40 years. In 1975 only 17% of the market capitalisation of the S&P 500 was vested in intangible assets. By 2015, this figure was 84%[6]. There is no longer necessarily a direct link between the use of natural resources and economic growth. Innovation is helping us to divorce what we own from what we earn.

2007 was also the year that the GFC started to bite and Apple released its first iPhone. Despite the GFC, this one product set Apple on a trajectory to become the world's biggest company. Smartphones have changed the way we live, but the way we work has not always kept up with the technology. In recent decades, the imperative to innovate has been clear, but not universally embraced. Some have seen innovation as 'nice to have', the domain of Silicon Valley darlings and tech start-ups. Risk-averse boards and CEOs have been reluctant to try anything too 'new'. Better to let someone else make the mistakes before us. It won't flood here.

The global financial impacts of 2020 have already surpassed those of the GFC. Technologies that we once saw as 'optional' are now essential. Health has become a collective concern, rather than solely an individual concern. Our connection to the environment has deepened. We can't live on 'the surface' anymore. Our need to innovate has become immediate and compelling.

---

6 Ocean Tomo LLC, 2015. Annual Study of Intangible Asset Market Value, Chicago: Ocean Tomo LLC.

2020 marks the end of complacency.
Innovation is not a luxury. It's an imperative.

2020 marks the end of complacency. Innovation is not a luxury. It's an imperative. Our very survival depends upon it. We have, now, an overwhelming opportunity to channel our resources, our collective wisdom and our human spirit into something bigger, something more enduring, something essential.

Anything pre-2020 has quickly become antediluvian. Like Noah, we now need to decide what we'll put on our ark and what we'll leave behind. Once we're on board, there's no going back, But the world looks brighter on the other side.

Beyond 2020

Survival is easy. It's our most powerful human instinct. People don't take much convincing to work for their own survival. When survival is no longer at stake, motivating people toward a common goal is hard. Not because the goal is too big, but because it's not big enough.

How do we emerge from 2020 stronger, healthier and more resilient than ever? How do we nurture sustainable growth rather than just struggle to survive?

Throughout much of history, he who owned the land had the power. Land equalled wealth. Wars were fought and kingdoms were built over the tiniest tracts of land, if they would yield a strategic advantage. In 2020 we've seen catastrophic drops in the value of many assets. Share markets have collapsed, superannuation funds have crumbled and house prices have plunged. What we own doesn't matter as much anymore.

My doctoral research [7], as well as more recent research I've conducted on the Top 100 ASX All Industrials [8], shows a clear connection between a company's innovation ethos and its growth trajectory [9]. A company with an owner ethos focuses on tangible capital assets and relies on passive capital growth for their returns. In the current environment, this capital growth is often negative and many owners face stranded asset risk.

By contrast, ideas as assets, which are purely intangible, provide potential for unconstrained growth [10]. This fits with a creator ethos. There is no theoretical limit on the number of times an idea can be sold. Creation of the idea itself requires relatively small capital investment. The required risk capacity is low and the potential return on investment is high. When looking to re-start growth after a catastrophic shock, ideas are our most essential assets. They provide the next step that will set us on our path for future growth. Beyond 2020 what we create is more important than what we own.

Pre-2020	Beyond 2020
What we own	What we create
Resources	Resilience

---

7 Beedles, M., 2002. The uncertain role of alliances in the strategic armoury of the dominant firms in the global pharmaceutical industry. Brisbane: QUT PhD Thesis.

8 Beedles, M. & Sheridan, M., 2015. Defining organisational performance: an asset management perspective. Sydney, Asset Management Council.

9 Beedles, M., 2019. The imperative for innovation in asset management. Fremantle, Asset Management Council.

10 ibid.

Pre-2020	Beyond 2020
Capital	Creativity
Individual Health	Collective Health
Innovation as a luxury	Innovation as an imperative

Green shoots

We know we need to innovate but it can be hard to know where, or when, to start. It may be tempting to wait till things get 'back to normal'. We need to accept that there's no going back. Instead, there's a different kind of normal. It may be counterintuitive to think that we can initiate innovation in the path of catastrophe, but the silt left by flood waters creates a rich and fertile environment to nourish fresh, green shoots.

There's a myth in Western culture about the hero scientist - Newton being struck by an apple, Archimedes leaping from the bath exclaiming Eureka! We can be led to believe that innovation requires a lightning bolt of genius inspiration. What if inspiration never strikes? This can feed a fear of failure and the perception that innovation is based on random chance and therefore perceived as high risk[11]. While there may be grains of truth in these stories, in reality lightning bolts don't come out of the blue. The storm has to brew first. On a summer afternoon the humidity builds, the sky darkens, rumbles echo in the distance, until the moment is right for the storm to break. Fear of failure can hold us back, but we have no need to be intimidated by these hero stories. Instead we can harness our inherent human ingenuity and create an environment in which it can flourish.

11 Beedles, M., 2020. Reducing the risks of innovation in asset management. Melbourne, Asset Management Council.

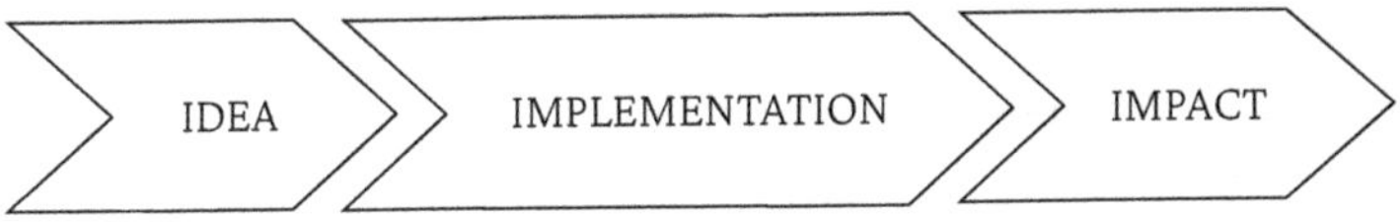

Figure 4: Idea to Impact

Ideas on their own are not innovation. Innovation creates value from ideas and this only happens when the ideas are implemented. An idea without implementation is just a thought bubble. Implementing innovation effectively requires commitment, consistency and collaboration. Of these, collaboration has been under most threat in recent times. In 2020, what we trust as 'safe' has changed and this has influenced the way we collaborate.

Lightning bolts don't come out of the blue. The storm has to brew first. On a summer afternoon the humidity builds, the sky darkens, rumbles echo in the distance, until the moment is right for the storm to break.

A few years ago, I worked with a company that had purpose built a fancy new open plan office to 'enhance collaboration'. When the teams moved to the new office, they no longer had walls between them but there were still barriers. It was amazing to see that those who didn't speak to each other before the move, still didn't speak to each other afterward. The physical walls had been replaced by 'invisible' walls, like a mime creeping their hands up an imaginary pane of glass.

Recent empirical research from Harvard Business School has shown that transitioning from a partitioned space to an open plan environment consistently reduces face-to-face interactions by about 70%[12]. Instead, email and instant messenger communication increases, as people feel it is 'safer' than talking out loud in a space where they may be overheard. To collaborate effectively, people don't need an open space, they need a safe space.

When we feel unsafe, we install barriers, like plastic screens at checkouts, ropes across communal areas and bollards at borders. By contrast, when we feel safe, we let down our guard and we open up to the possibilities and opportunities that true collaboration brings. What we've seen recently is that if we create a safe space, even oceans, or flood waters, are no barrier to connection and collaboration. We've found new ways to maintain and enhance our interactions across physical and geographical boundaries.

In 2020 scientists around the world have been collaborating at an escalating scale and pace. The imperative to quickly share information has set aside the traditional paths to publishing scientific research findings and has seen platforms such as pre-print servers inundated with early stage results[13]. Such research has not yet been peer reviewed in the manner of traditional scientific publications, but it provides other researchers with access to this information to guide their own investigations. Prestigious journals, such as the New England Journal of Medicine have published papers in as little as 48 hours[14], a process that would normally take several years.

---

12 Bernstein, E. & Turban, S., 2018. The impact of the 'open' workspace on human collaboration. Philosophical Transactions of The Royal Society B, 373(20170239).

13 upferschmidt, K., 2020. 'A completely new culture of doing research.' Coronavirus outbreak changes how scientists communicate. Science, 26 Feb.

14 ibid.

Dr. Ryan Carroll, a Harvard Medical professor has observed that big, exclusive research can lead to grants, promotions and tenure, so scientists often work in secret, suspiciously hoarding data from potential competitors. *"The ability to work collaboratively, setting aside your personal academic progress, is occurring right now because it's a matter of survival,"* he said[15].

Scientists can discuss their findings with each other via platforms such as slack and twitter, transcending national barriers and overlooking the usual secrecy that surrounds results prior to publication[16]. From its first submission in December 2019, the Global Initiative on Sharing All Influenza Data *(GISAID)* has to the end of May 2020 received more than 35,000 submissions of viral genome sequence data from around the world[17], enabling rapid, real-time progress in understanding essential viral features needed for testing, tracing and evaluation of interventions.

For collaboration to be purposeful it requires a conscious decision and deliberate effort to bring people together who might normally pass in the hall. There needs to be a visible commitment to empower innovation. This includes commitment of funds and allocation of time for innovation activities. It also means adopting a consistent approach to innovate every day, rather than one-off or occasional activities. Ad hoc innovation leads to ad hoc results. As we emerge from physical isolation towards more face-to-face, but carefully controlled interaction, we need to be mindful of how we consciously commit to creating consistent opportunities for meaningful collaboration.

---

15 Apuzzo, M. & Kirkpatrick, D., 2020. Covid-19 Changed How the World Does Science, Together. The New York Times, 1 April.

16 ibid.

17 GISAID Initiative, 2020. GISAID Initiative. [Online] Available at: https://www.gisaid.org/

We are now considering how life and work will change as we move into a 'recovery' phase. Trust is important as we choose who we'll meet with face-to-face, which public places we'll go to and when we'll return to the office, or use public transport. Many aspects of life that we once took for granted have now become weighty decisions, with an inbuilt risk analysis before we tentatively step beyond our own front door.

As we return to events, how many people can fit? What will staffing and cleaning costs be? Will insurance cover us if someone gets sick? Restaurants are becoming more like railways, focussed on reducing 'dwell time' and keeping people moving. For leaders many of the questions remain the same as they have ever been. How do we create value while balancing risk and compliance obligations? As the world has changed, does our value proposition still stack up? If not, what do we need to do?

What's next?

History doesn't repeat, but it rhymes. Unplanned changes are a part of life. Some are minor and some are more significant, but change of some kind is inevitable. It's not what happens in our lives, but how we respond that determines our outcomes. If we realise that innovation is an imperative, not a luxury, we can make a positive start towards the future we see for ourselves.

We may be tempted to throw our well-made plans out the window if what we once owned is gone. We can focus instead, not on what we've lost, but on what we can now create. Through commitment, consistency and collaboration, we can nurture an environment that allows our most valuable ideas to flourish. We can adapt where we have to, without abandoning our core desires and values. As we take our first steps into the wet silt, let's hold onto those things that matter most and build our ark around them.

Summary:

Innovation is not a luxury. It's an imperative.

What we create matters more than what we own.

Successful innovation requires commitment, consistency, and collaboration.

Questions:

1. To what level has your business been disrupted?
2. How important is innovation for your business?
3. How risky is innovation for you?
4. How effective is your collaboration?
5. How confident do you feel in implementing innovation?

About the Author:

Dr. Monique Beedles

Dr Monique Beedles has always been excited by innovation. She started her career in the pharmaceutical industry working in research, manufacturing and hospitals. This was an industry with a clear imperative to innovate. Monique pursued her PhD in Corporate Strategy to better understand how companies make the strategic decisions that enable innovation. 20 years on, every industry has an imperative to innovate.

Monique is the author of two books, Pivot Point: making the decisions that matter in business and Asset Management for Directors. In her work with boards and executive teams, Monique is passionate about reducing the risks of innovation to improve company performance and create real value for stakeholders. Monique's IDEAS 365 Program supports leaders to implement innovation into the daily work of their teams, to reduce risk, keep control and remain relevant.

CHAPTER THREE

Design

Jennifer Kenny

Paul Polman, the co-founder of sustainability consulting firm, IMAGINE, and the former CEO of Unilever, wrote a lovely, hopeful piece in the Harvard Business Review in May 2020.

> "*As COVID-19 continues its advance, it is showing that much that we believed was wrong. Things that seemed impossible a few months ago have suddenly come to pass. As it turns out, thousands of businesses, universities, and other organizations can pivot to a totally virtual environment in days, not years. Societies divided by politics and inequality can quickly come together in shows of mass solidarity. The pollution over China can magically disappear.*"[1]

1 Polman, P., Sisodia, R. and Tindell, K., 2020. What Good Business Looks Like. [online] Available at: <https://hbr.org/2020/05/what-good-business-looks-like> [Accessed 13 May 2020].

These are days for challenging and changing dogma.

The crisis is forcing us to do things we've never done before, in ways we've never done before.

A lot of these changes, like the examples cited by Polman in his article, are positive ones. But as we develop policy on the fly, we risk getting a lot wrong too: making a lot of mistakes, creating a lot of waste, and leaving people behind as we innovate and respond to the changes happening around us.

The pandemic has given us an appetite for innovation, and new ways of thinking. It seems people are wary of 'more of the same' - including innovating the same old flawed way we have in the past. We are already predisposed to doing things in a way that is more engaging, humane, interconnected and mutually compassionate and respectful. People are looking to be heard and to participate actively in the design of a better world, and create a better future for all of us.

Over the years of leading large-scale transformation projects with Fortune 500s and others, there is one particular approach for leading innovation that I have found to be well-suited to the current times: Design Thinking.

Design Thinking is particularly helpful for:

- challenging and changing the dogma,
- supporting us through what could be the biggest transformation of society and work in our lifetimes, and
- helping us lead others to a better future.

To truly understand Design Thinking, we need to see the outcomes it can create.

Meet The Bank Where Culture and Communication Stifled Innovation

Several years ago, I was working for one of America's largest banks. Their commercial banking, loan document processing group were struggling with what seemed to be gross inefficiency, and they were losing deals and customers at an alarming rate.

There were two very different groups on either side of the loan sales process:

- The Commercial Bankers: predominantly male, white, middle class, college-educated, English as a first language, suburban dwellers, extroverts, and;
- The Document Processors: predominantly female, people of color or other marginalized groups, high school educated, lower middle class or working class, English as a second language or first-generation English speakers, urban dwellers, introverts.

(Generalization, but you get the picture.)

Both groups were frustrated at what they saw as the deficiencies of the others, how it impacted performance, communication, and morale, and ultimately the division's ability to innovate solutions.

A lack of empathy kept pushing these two groups apart, preventing them from collaborating and innovating.

This is where Design Thinking was able to help us to break an impasse.

What Is Design Thinking?

As an innovation methodology, Design Thinking was first developed by Terry Winograd and Larry Leifer in 2005 at the design school at Stanford University. In its relatively short existence, the methodology quickly gained widespread adoption by highly innovative companies worldwide.

According to Tim Brown, CEO of IDEO - one of the pioneering agencies who popularised the methodology - Design Thinking is *"an approach that uses the designers' sensibilities and methods for problem-solving to meet people's needs in a technologically feasible and commercially viable way."*

Unlike problem-based thinking *(which tends to fixate on problems and obstacles)*, Design Thinking is an approach to complex problem solving that focuses on user outcomes and favours experimentation. It creates opportunities for innovation that may sidestep problems completely, and involves an iterative process of continued improvement. All of these factors make it well-suited to the complexity, ambiguity and volatility that we find ourselves in as a result of the pandemic.

We can apply Design Thinking to the design and development of products - but also to designing and developing the way we work. This includes improving the human interactions needed to create great products, experiences and customer outcomes.

In other words, Design Thinking can apply both to the design of things and the design of cultures of innovation in any company, team or project.

The 3 Phases of Design Thinking

There are three phases of Design Thinking:

1. Inspiration
2. Ideation
3. Implementation

Phase 1: Inspiration

At its core, Design Thinking understands the role of people in all business processes:

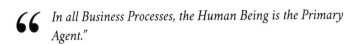

> “*In all Business Processes, the Human Being is the Primary Agent.*”

The key to unlocking inspiration in this first phase of Design Thinking is empathy.

My team and I were working with a division of a major global computer software and hardware manufacturing and development company. They were committed to shifting to a more services-oriented company and moving away from their manufacturing and hardware base. Our job was to help them move from order takers of hardware to consultative sellers of services – a significant change in mindset. We were prototyping with a pilot team.

I was coaching one of the senior executives one day, and he confided in me that his wife and daughters liked him more now that he knew how to listen. He was almost in tears; the emotional relief of being recognized for being empathetic with people he loved was so overwhelming. He had begun to embody what we were doing at work and without any input from me *(I was not coaching him on his personal life)* had taken this new practise of becoming empathy-led home. With that level of embodiment and commitment, I knew that we had substantially increased the chances of success and sustainability for our work. This pilot team went from the bottom on the list in sales to being #1 in the region.

The core of empathy is how you use language. Through empathy, we can develop deeper understanding, unlock a deeper level of communication, and have greater impact.

Empathy is a hugely powerful *(and often overlooked)* tool for eliciting change within an organization.

Back to our story about the bank - one of the biggest issues facing this division was a lack of empathy.

The two groups on either side of the commercial lending division - the predominantly white, male, college-educated Commercial Bankers; and the predominantly female, marginalized, high-school educated Document Processors - were clashing culturally at their cores.

If we had taken a problem-based approach to this issue, we might have hired an expert on team culture and empathy. But it would have taken us decades to help them empathize with each other if we had started with teaching them about empathy and then asked them to practice that at work. They might have thought that it was fascinating and relevant and inspiring, but they would have promptly forgotten it as soon as the next fire drill happened, and someone started yelling at someone else.

Instead we introduced them to a pragmatic branch of Design Thinking called the Language/Action Perspective *(LAP)* which effectively shows people how to enact and practice agency: action by a human being to produce their desired outcome.

The LAP leverages language to help people become designers of their own lives.

Language is the most powerful and effective aspect of being human. According to Terry Winograd *(the Stanford Professor who coined both Design Thinking, and Language/Action Perspective)*: *"Language is action. Through their linguistic acts people effect change in the world."* [2]

Language is the most significant evolutionary advantage that separates us from our ancestors. Without language, we might be able to develop empathy, but it would take a very long time, we would not be able to do much else at the same time, and we would certainly not be able to find design solutions to complex problems. We couldn't create opportunities, negotiate outcomes or collaborate on innovative solutions.

By utilizing the LAP, the Commercial Bankers and Document Processors were able to develop a new, shared cultural framework for communication. In a sense, they were able to speak the same

---

2 Winograd, T., 2006. Designing a new foundation for design. Communications of the ACM, 49(5), p.71.

language. And for the first time, this allowed them to gain a deep and empathetic understanding of the problems they were facing.

This was the first Design Thinking step towards innovating a new approach to working inside the bank's commercial lending division.

Phase 2: Ideation

Although empathy is an important starting point for innovation - giving us the Inspiration we need to understand the nature of problems deeply - Inspiration itself doesn't innovate.

Instead, we build on the Inspiration we developed in Phase 1 of the Design Thinking process, beginning Ideation of solutions.

Firmly rooted in our understanding of the customer, their agency and their position in the hierarchy of processes, we can begin to speculate how to serve the customer better. At the same time, we must remember that the network of conversations happens both inside and outside the company. We must also not forget that conversations between humans do not always acknowledge the boundaries constructed to define individual companies, customers, or employees.

With this foundation, we begin to recognize, design and model conversations to produce customer satisfaction in every conversation that we have both inside and outside the company. People become transformed from 'inbox processors' with mind-numbing tasks for disembodied managers and departments to being human designers and performers of requests, offers and mutual promises to other human beings. The human, or social, work gains meaning where goals, visions, and a desire to satisfy human customers, comes to life.

Once we have this solidly in place, we enter into the magical realm of co-invention. The Design Thinking model refers to this as 'ideate'. But as anyone who has done ideation knows, the result is only as good as the participants' level of mutual trust and willingness to play and learn together.

I call this the magical realm because this is really where the magic happens, again and again. This realm is where human beings get to invent something better together. And where we have fun and really get to know each other. By 'knowing each other', I'm not talking about knowing what someone's dog ate for breakfast or the names and ages of their kids, but knowing how another person thinks; what they value; how they see the world; what matters to them and how we can engage in delivering value for each other.

The bank now had a shared understanding of the problems being faced through the LAP. The Commercial Bankers and the Document Processors were able to negotiate, together designing shared standards for creating customer satisfaction for each other and for their customers. They were ultimately able to develop empathy by listening well enough to each other to collaborate and build trust.

The Document Processors developed a sufficient level of agency that they gained the respect of the Commercial Bankers. The combined group's customer satisfaction ratings jumped 11%[3], unheard of in the history of the measurements.

3 As measure by the bank's independent audit group

Best of all, at least for me, one of the Document Processors confided in me that she no longer cried on the way to work. That's empathy in the trenches. All good design begins with empathy.

However, to say that Inspiration and Ideation alone got them there is to gloss over perhaps the most important step in the Design Thinking process - *Implementation.*

Phase 3: Implementation

Knowing that we are looking to change behaviors and practices, and ultimately mindsets and cultures, heavily informs the Inspiration and Ideation phases.

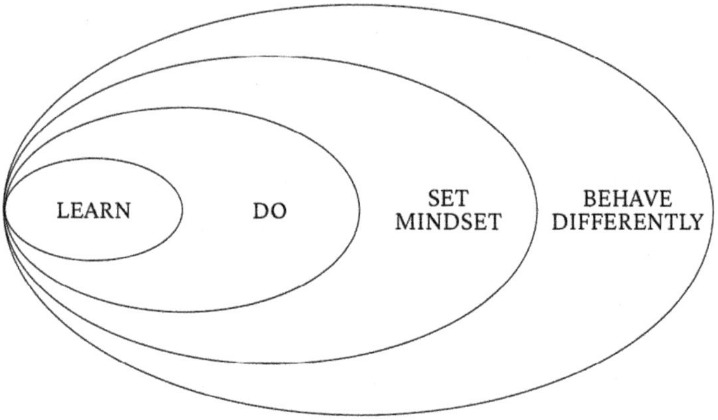

Figure 5: Shifting Behaviors and Practices

When we are trying to change behaviours and practices inside an organisation, the thing that is hardest to change, and requires the most rethinking, IS the people. Human-centered design inside an organisation often requires changes in the way humans think, behave and act.

But whether or not we're rethinking people, policy, product or procedures our Implementation needs to involve, inspire and mobilize people. If we fail to design for mobilization, our Design Thinking projects and programs are not human-centered design, they are manufacturing input-process-output applied with wishful thinking to humans.

At the beginning of this chapter, I shared a quote from the Harvard Business Review, where Paul Polman wrote about how the pandemic has seen thousands of businesses, universities and other organisations pivot towards a digital future in days, not years - how societies divided by politics quickly rallied in solidarity - and how impossible pollution problems could magically disappear.

These outcomes would not have been possible if it weren't for a huge mobilization of people. Through mobilization, the impossible can be achieved.

For the horrific cost that the pandemic has taken on humankind at large, one positive we can take from this is that it has accelerated our pace of innovation - giving us a new appetite for change, and a new willingness to adopt it.

It's crucial that we allow people the opportunity to be heard, and actively participate in the design of a new and better world. There's a desire to design better ways of doing things, a process that we can take to unlock these better ways, and a better future ahead for all of us if we can do this.

Summary:

People have a strong appetite for innovation right now - and are eager to be mobilized to address the issues around COVID-19.

Business-as-usual is risky. People want to be involved in designing their own futures, and innovating solutions to COVID-19. Nobody wants to be left behind.

Design Thinking is a high-empathy human-centered methodology for innovation that is well suited to the volatility, complexity and uncertainty of the current times.

Questions:

1. In the wake of COVID-19, what brighter future can you imagine for your role, your organization, your industry, or the world at large?
2. Who are the key people involved in creating these brighter futures?
3. INSPIRATION: How can you engage people *(deeply, and with empathy)* who are involved in creating these futures - and gain deep insight into the issues?
4. IDEATION: How can you collaborate with these people to ideate new innovations, processes, and experiences?
5. IMPLEMENTATION: How can you involve and mobilize as many people around these innovative new solutions as possible?

About the Author:

Jennifer Kenny

Jennifer Kenny is a master of innovation practices. She increases the capacity of leaders, teams and organizations to fuel innovation, performance and revenue in complex and emergent technology ecosystems. Jennifer is passionate about helping amazing people deliver highly successful projects by amplifying others.

For more than 25 years, Jennifer has devoted herself to the study and practice of innovation. Building on the disciplines of Systems Thinking, Language Action Design and Human Coordination she has developed the Mastering the Innovation Mindset© and Mastering Innovation Leadership© programs to help senior leaders and their teams ignite and embed transformative innovation practices. These programs provide critical meta-skills, methodologies and frameworks that enable them to lead and amplify cross-functional innovation capabilities, rapidly develop more valuable products and optimal coordination processes.

Jennifer graduated from University College, Dublin with a B.Sc. in geology and chemistry, has an M.Sc. in engineering geology from Imperial College, London and a Masters in Innovation from the Center for Innovation Leadership at Stanford Research Institute.

Today, she works with the biggest names in tech and offers transformative leadership development to research and development teams around the world.

Preparing for the Journey

Not being able to see where the path leads, the hero gathers tools she thinks will help her on the journey.

PURPOSE

CHAPTER FOUR

Purpose

Darin Fox

You could hear the proverbial pin drop.

The silence in the crowded room was broken only by the bubbling of the large silver percolators of coffee, gasping as if they were expressing their shock and horror at my impertinent question.

The uncomfortable silence was momentary. What followed was arguably worse – whispering neighbour turned to neighbour amongst the hushed rows of my fellow HR professionals; invited to meet the presenting author. I sat alone, staring at the speaker, hoping for an answer to my question but waited through the hushed whispers of disbelief, the low murmuring outcry of offence and the awkward glance of people who looked at me as if I was the first stranger who entered their home town in 20 years.

"Could purpose trump culture?"

I thought my question to the guest presenter was simple and straightforward, but apparently, it bordered on blasphemy.

I had been thinking about the question myself for some time prior. The presenter spoke about his new book regarding the leadership skills required in an environment of increasing complexity and uncertainty. One of his fundamental tenets was that this same environment was making culture much more difficult to manage. It was not asked entirely out of context. It was not as if I came to disrupt, to defile or profane. My question was relevant.

The speaker circled around my question with enviable skill. He didn't affirm my question in the positive; nor did he reject it. He had read the room, and he was there to sell his book after all. I took his lack of outright rejection of my violation among the pious as a quiet nod of support. If his safety was not at risk, then surely a few book sales were lost by those who expected him to cast me back to the bottomless pit of hell from where I spawned.

At the end of the presentation, I escaped quietly and quickly. I forewent the sun-dried tomato mini muffins, and the gluten-free mini scones, convinced I had stumbled upon something important.

As I walked out the door, I swore I heard the percolators give me one final self-righteous hiss. To me, it was the whisper that launched a personal revolution.

***

That was late 2018. Since then, the question has become a conviction. Purpose does indeed trump culture. My faith is grounded in 20 years of playing the culture change lottery and seeing how purpose evens the odds. Furthermore, purpose being your trump card over culture is even more evident as we make our tentative first steps into a post-COVID, new-normal world.

I am not suggesting you should ignore your culture. However, the vast majority of organisations and leaders ignore their purpose, and they do so with an increasing hazard and lost opportunity. The level of resources spent on changing culture often goes beyond the point of diminishing returns, and those extra resources are better utilised in protecting and embedding the organisation's purpose. Too often, a focus on purpose is a singular event; a poster on a wall launched with much ado and fanfare but embedded with little more than the occasional screensaver and mouse pad.

A search on Amazon for business books about purpose returns almost 4000 listings. Management god Peter Drucker has been writing about purpose since the 1970s. Simon Sinek's book *"Start with Why"*[1] almost kicked purpose into the realm of pop culture and then his TEDx Talk[2], with more than 50 million views, punted it into the

1 Sinek, S., 2009. Start With Why.

2 "simon sinek start with why | TEDx.|" https://www.ted.com/talks/simon_sinek_how_great_leaders_inspire_action?language=en

next stadium. Dan Pontefract's *"The Purpose Effect"*[3] provides readers with an instruction manual for finding and embedding purpose. Daniel Pink in his book 'Drive: The surprising truth about what motivates us'[4] writes that science states there are three key drivers of motivation: autonomy, mastery and purpose; and suggests that of the three, purpose makes the most significant difference.

Purpose, in theory, is easy to say, and evidently even easier to write a book about. Unfortunately, it is tougher to do. The daily minutia of managing cost centres, approvals and bureaucracy often sees purpose easily forgotten. In a crisis, it's often thrown out the corner office window. ALSO TASKY OR PROCESSORS

Your purpose is your why

Purpose is your reason for being. It is not your products or the services you provide. Instead, your purpose is the positive difference your product or service will make in the world, and it is the criteria you use to decide which products and services you will produce. A defined purpose is bigger than you and your organisation, and exists outside of it. In his commencement address to Harvard graduates in 2017, Mark Zuckerberg said *"Purpose is that sense that we are part of something bigger than ourselves."*[5] For the same reason, your purpose should not even be specific to your industry.

For example, here are three corporate purposes. Are you able to pinpoint the industry these organisations act?

---

3 Pontefract, D., 2018. The Purpose Effect. La Vergne: Figure 1 Publishing.

4 Pink, D., 2009. Drive. New York: Riverhead Books

5 "Mark Zuckerberg's speech as written for Harvard's Class of 2017." 25 May. 2017, https://news.harvard.edu/gazette/story/2017/05/mark-zuckerbergs-speech-as-written-for-harvards-class-of-2017/.

1. 'Together we can change the way the world does business.'

2. 'To make your world a safer place.'

3. 'To help people live more fulfilling and productive working lives and help organisations succeed.'[6]

Providing clarity of purpose for what the organisation stands for, and the *"why"* that will motivate its people to dedicate their efforts, might be the most crucial activity a business leader needs to undertake now. More than ever before, leaders will need to inject purpose into the DNA of their organisation.

So why now?

It may still be too early to predict any societal changes from COVID but we are heading towards a new normal. Even if an effective vaccine is found, then *"normal"* will still not be a return to everything as it once was. If a vaccine is not found, or not made available to the whole global population, then we are heading for substantial changes indeed.

We can make some safe predictions based on history, psychology and by extrapolating current trends. People will become exhausted by ongoing uncertainty and gravitate towards anyone who offers a return to a certain and secure future. Leaders who provide simple but shallow answers will find customers for their snake-oil, but people will flock to purpose-driven leaders who can point to their North Star through the storm.

---

6 The companies and industries are Unilever (Consumer Goods), IAG (Insurance), and Seek.com (Recruitment)

It is likely we will become suspicious of those we deem not like us. There is a large body of research, most notably Thornhill and Fincher's *"The Parasite-Stress Theory of Values and Sociality"*[7] showed that people who live in areas of high infection rates are much more likely to state they don't want neighbours from a different race or speak a different language. We should expect less globalisation and more shop-local. A strong purpose-driven leader may be able to nudge this trend into a more positive direction of higher communal values and decreasing self-centredness. If any good comes from COVID, I hope at least we see the hero worship of fame and wealth is replaced by an appreciation of those who make sacrifices for the community.

The sense of personal agency will decrease as global trends well beyond the control of any government, let alone an individual, cause unpredictable changes to our lifestyle. A purpose-driven leader can give back a sense of control over destiny by empowering people to apply their strengths to a higher purpose. It is likely young people, more than ever, will be attracted to those organisations which offer such an opportunity as shown by research by the London Business School[8], PWC[9], Deloitte[10] and many others.

The greater the complexity and uncertainty an organisation faces, the more critical its purpose becomes. Purpose is your North Star. It can be the unchanging reference point to guide you back to your destination when the journey becomes treacherous. Culture, profits,

---

7 Thornhill, R. and Fincher, C., 2014. The parasite-stress theory of sociality, the behavioral immune system, and human social and cognitive uniqueness. Evolutionary Behavioral Sciences, 8(4), pp.257-264.

8 "Most millennials will only work for purpose-driven firms ...." 29 Mar. 2018, https://www.london.edu/news/most-millennials-will-only-work-for-purpose-driven-firms-1431.

9 PwC, 2018. "Workforce of the future - The Yellow World in 2030: PwC."

10 Deloitte, 2017. "Deloitte Global Human Capital Trends"

revenue, sales, and customer feedback can all fluctuate. Your purpose does not shift unless you allow it to. In the face of adversity, an organization's purpose is simultaneously put to the ultimate test while also being its greatest asset.

Your purpose trumps your culture. From an anthropological perspective, all culture is learned behaviour that evolves through interactions between people as they first determine what is required to survive around here. Once survival is relatively guaranteed, they learn what is necessary to thrive in good times and through the storms. A culture can be 'managed' by leaders consciously leading through example, nudging behaviours in the correct direction, and by building systems and processes which encourage the right behaviour. Ultimately, culture takes form in the interaction between people, and between people and their environment.

What will happen when the frequency of those interactions reduces significantly due to ongoing social distancing and remote working? How is culture *"managed"* when the medium of those interactions occurs across a computer screen? How do leaders nudge behaviour when the frequency of meetings is reduced, and meeting rooms are too small to allow everyone to participate while social distancing? The answer in the new normal will demand purpose. Organisations of purpose, with all their people empowered to enact it every day, will be those who will thrive through the storm.

> " *There are decades where nothing happens; and there are weeks where decades happen." - Vladimir Lenin*

COVID may have fanned the flames, but the shift from profit to purpose has been a slow burn since the GFC in 2008.

Since 2008, business leaders, management gurus and academics have been promoting the role of purpose in business, and that effort should be directed beyond profits to improving the community it operates in. An article in the MIT Sloan Management Review in January 2018 wrote that Friedman's view of business is no longer valid, and increasing complexity and uncertainty make the focus on quarterly profits unsustainable.[11]

The US Business Roundtable, a lobbying group of 200 CEOs from some of the biggest companies in the world issued a joint statement in 2019 on *"the purpose of a corporation"*, writing that *"companies should no longer advance only the interests of shareholders."* Instead, *"they must also invest in their employees, protect the environment, and deal fairly and ethically with their suppliers"*.[12]

Larry Fink, the CEO and chairperson of BlackRock, a global investment management firm that managed more than $6 trillion in assets titled his 2018 annual letter to global CEOs *"A Sense of Purpose."* [13]

This wasn't supposed to happen, according to Economic Theory. Milton Friedman's 1970 article *"The Social Responsibility of Business is to Increase its Profits"* in the New York Times[14] is often cited as

11 "The Social Responsibility of Business Is to Create Value for ...." 4 Jan. 2018, https://sloanreview.mit.edu/article/the-social-responsibility-of-business-is-to-create-value-for-stakeholders/. Accessed 4 Jul. 2020.

12 "Business Roundtable Redefines the Purpose of a Corporation ...." 19 Aug. 2019, https://www.businessroundtable.org/business-roundtable-redefines-the-purpose-of-a-corporation-to-promote-an-economy-that-serves-all-americans.

13 "Larry Fink's Letter to CEOs | BlackRock." https://www.blackrock.com/corporate/investor-relations/larry-fink-ceo-letter.

14 Friedman, M., 1970. The Social Responsibility of Business is to Increase its Profits. New York Times Magazine.

the doctrine that launched an ideology that business exists solely to maximise shareholder value. We have all seen how fundamentally flawed that view is and the problems it has caused, not the least of which was the Global Financial Crisis.

Purpose and performance

Purpose is no longer an empty slogan, spewed from the board room table because tradition dictates organisations need vision and purpose statements. Purpose is now a competitive differentiator, and those companies which treat it as such and embed it as a way of working are those that tend to succeed more than others.

Rick Wartzman wrote in Fortune Magazine, *"...building a deep and authentic sense of purpose could be a company's ultimate competitive advantage."*[15] Forbes magazine has also contributed significant and accessible business research into the competitive value of purpose.

An American study by Cone & Porter Novelli in 2018 found almost all companies *(83%)* that beat the market in revenue growth have a clearly articulated purpose.[16]

Quarterly earnings reports do not drive a purpose-driven organisation. They are focused on the long game. McKinsey Global Institute showed firms focusing their business on the long term had

---

15 "What Unilever shares with Google and Apple | Fortune." https://fortune.com/2015/01/07/what-unilever-shares-with-google-and-apple/.

16 Cone/Porter Novelli, 2018. 2018 Cone/Porter Novelli Purpose Study. Boston.

47 per cent higher revenues, 36 per cent higher net income and added 12,000 more jobs on average.[17]

Deloitte reported purpose-first organisations *"have 30 per cent higher levels of innovation and 40 per cent higher levels of retention, and they tend to be first or second in their market segment."*[18]

If an organisation's purpose is meaningful and credible, if it commits to solving real problems to make its community a better place, then it will build trust because the purpose is authentic and not just a poster on the wall. Real purpose will drive loyalty in customers and employees. Yet there is so much more to a purpose than the poster. Every aspect of an organisation must be aligned so that its people can enact the purpose every day. The Harvard Business Review's *"Business Case for Purpose"* found executives almost unanimously agreed that purpose drives performance, but only half of those interviewed had a clearly articulated purpose. Then, among them, only a small handful of companies have fully embedded their purpose in their organisations to the point of delivering higher performance.[19]

The how of why

Most organisations have a documented purpose, as well as a vision, values, and culture statements. But to obtain the benefits of a purpose, it must become part of the daily workflow. Leaders must be committed to living the purpose and ensuring that every aspect

---

17 McKinsey Global Institute, 2017. Measuring The Economic Impact Of Short-Termism. McKinsey and Company, p.7.

18 "A new model for employee engagement | Deloitte Insights." 27 Jan. 2015, https://www2.deloitte.com/us/en/insights/deloitte-review/issue-16/employee-engagement-strategies.html.

19 Harvard Business Review, 2020. The Business Case For Purpose. Harvard Business Review, p.1.

of the organisation — from role descriptions, recruitment decisions, onboarding, policies, and commercial decision-making criteria have the purpose at its core. Unless it is integrated into the day-to-day, you don't have a purpose. You have a poster on a wall. If your organisation pays higher performance bonuses for those who achieve the highest sales or profit and not for the achievement of your purpose, then you don't have a purpose. If you don't recruit people who are motivated and passionate about your purpose, then you don't have a purpose.

Purpose is hard work, but it can be your competitive advantage if you treat it as such. That means empowering every employee to apply their strengths towards that competitive advantage.

Purpose has to start with each employee and not as a glib statement launched from the executive team. It begins with each person empowered to align their purpose with the organisation. Sometimes that means talented people may leave, but there is a reason why leadership coaches and organisational therapists start out exploring their clients' purpose. Sam Ferres, a Rapid Transformational Therapy coach, helps female entrepreneurs to be more successful in their businesses. The first step in her e-book *"Mindset Success in 5 steps"* asks the reader to explore and articulate their purpose before doing anything else.[20]

Purpose trumps culture. If you genuinely embed purpose to the point your people can enact that purpose every day, then you can achieve more outcomes than a culture change program would produce. Now, in our uncertain post-COVID new-normal world, your purpose will make those outcomes even more likely because a North Star allows your people to course correct themselves. Psychologists know that

20 Ferres, Samantha, 2020. "Mindset Change in Just 5 Steps e-book", https://www.dropbox.com/l/scl/AAA7lylAR8dvAGp02CXwW9qhU9AfdUaGcsI

a strong sense of purpose can give us focus and tenacity while also protecting us from anxiety and fear. We become less self-centred because we feel a part of something bigger. Purpose can improve our confidence and resilience. Purpose gives us hope.

Well before Milton Friedman, Economist Adam Smith wrote *"The Wealth of Nations"*.[21] In Chapter One, he used a pin factory to explain the division of labour - the reduction of any job into a series of specialised parts - as the engine of economic gain, and self-interest as oil for the engine. That pin factory was the foundation of economic theory for the next 200 years until now.

Can you hear the pin drop? It is the sound of revolution.

21 Smith, A., 1981. The Wealth Of Nations. London: Dent, p.7.

Summary:

Prolonged social distancing and remote working is going to make the already difficult process of managing culture almost impossible. Organisational purpose is where leaders should focus to align and engage their people.

Purpose is becoming a competitive advantage. Those who do purpose well, perform better.

To obtain benefits from organisational purpose, employees must be empowered to deliver the purpose every day. It has to be part of their every day workflow.

Questions:

1. Attraction – Is your purpose clearly written into your EVP marketing? Can candidates articulate your purpose?
2. Recruitment – Does your selection profile assess purpose-fit, and not just culture-fit? Do you hire people who show little evidence of being motivated by your purpose?
3. Rewards – to what extent do you financially reward people for clearly achieving the purpose of your organisation
4. Strategy – Does your executive team put the organisation's purpose as the core decision criteria for new products, services or strategic direction?
5. Engagement – Do you assess to what extent purpose motivates your people to go beyond the expectations of their role?

About the Author:

Darin Fox

Darin is a purpose-driven leader in organisational capability, workforce strategy and transformation who is passionate about building environments for people and teams to bring the best versions of themselves. Prior to joining HFL in 2020 as Principal Consultant and Chief Research Officer, Darin was a senior HR leader in banking, finance, telecommunications and utilities, developing and embedding future-ready enterprise workforce strategies. Darin's methodology quickly assesses an organisation's internal and external drivers, short and long-term commercial requirements and global workforce trends to develop holistic strategies which have led or supported M&A, divestments, workforce transformation, and new business. As a result of COVID, Darin is also a Dungeon Master in a weekly online game of Dungeons and Dragons with his 12-year old son, four boys in Sydney and three in Canada.

LANGUAGE WITH CERTAIN PROFESSIONAL
DEVELOPERS AS

CHAPTER FIVE

Shift

Andrew Deering

Abbie was the kind of leader you wished you had. The kind of colleague you could always rely upon. The kind of person you couldn't help but admire.

A successful leader in a senior corporate role, she was highly respected, and had a reputation for excellence and delivery.

Abbie thrived on challenge. She was used to managing complex situations and solving imposing problems.

But times of crisis have a way of upsetting the balance of even the most effective leaders.

It was the perfect storm of events - in both her personal, and professional life - that came crashing over Abbie. It left her disoriented, struggling to find the mastery and balance she once held.

In the midst of crisis, Abbie lost the sense of direction, focus, and control that had served her so well - and it wasn't clear how she could ever regain what she'd lost.

Right now, I imagine you're able to relate to Abbie in one way or another. Perhaps in multiple aspects of your life or one particular area, there's a lot of noise, activity, opinion, or even confusion.

Maybe it's useful for you to know that you're not alone.

For leaders, the potential of crisis is constant.

A study by PwC found 69% of business leaders had faced an organisational crisis in the years between 2014-2019 - and those were relatively smooth years.[1] During macro events, like pandemics and global financial crises, we can expect this number to be 100%!

As our world becomes increasingly globalized, interconnected, and complex - and economic, social, environmental and political pressures continue to rise - challenges of all shapes and sizes are becoming more common. And these challenges are having more wide-reaching impacts - throwing our work, our lives, and even our health out of balance.

---

1 https://www.pwc.com/gx/en/forensics/global-crisis-survey/pdf/pwc-global-crisis-survey-2019.pdf]

With crisis being a constant risk , it's more important than ever that leaders develop the skills necessary to be able to navigate uncertainty and complexity.

We require useful approaches to develop our people, manage ourselves, and reignite our businesses *(and more broadly humanity)* to face new and increasingly difficult challenges.

We need to be able to find and create potential and possibilities worth focusing on whenever dark clouds roll in.

We need to be able to create space, focus and clarity in times of confusion and complexity.

In short, we need to be able to create a *"Useful Shift"*.

Useful

One of the compliments I hold in the highest esteem is when someone says they found my work *"useful"* - and usefulness is the starting point in creating a Useful Shift.

While it may seem like a plain and utilitarian word, *"useful"* is earthy and profound.

When something is useful, it holds a depth of application. Useful things are pragmatic and practical. Useful things are uniquely able to create change, evolution, or improvement. It's why a carpenter will keep his most useful tools closest at hand, and why a leader will keep her most useful insights front-of-mind.

For leaders, the insights that are most useful to us tend to be the ones that help us to access possibilities we couldn't access before - and the ones that help us to discern between the possibilities that serve us and those that don't.

As a tool, the lens of usefulness helps us to do both of these things - to magnify, and to focus.

In its expansive sense, useful work has the power to compound, to grow, and to evolve because of the very fact it is utilitarian. It's effective, easy to understand, and easy to apply - and the practical nature of useful work is that it creates a domino effect, where growth and value are able to gather potentially boundless momentum for the individual or the collective.

In its pragmatic sense, usefulness also adds an extra layer of discernment to any decision you make, encouraging you to be intelligent, selective, and honest. Many wasteful decisions are made in business. We are easily distracted by the pretty *(shiny and distracting)*, the pointless *(things that require a lot of energy but don't get to the heart of the matter)*, and the precious *(things that appear great but crack under pressure)*. Every day, there are myriad decisions you and your organisation could make. But are they useful? Do they serve you and add value? This is the challenge our businesses, governments, and even countries face.

Now more than ever, we need to do useful things. If all we did day in, day out was useful – useful thoughts, activities, decisions, and conversations – we could move forward in a way that was meaningful, timely, and impactful. We would enable a Useful Shift.

When a crisis crashes over us, it can damage our sense of direction, focus and control - the very senses that help us to discern the useful from the useless.

We needed to create new landmarks for navigating the complex and uncertain waters of Abbie's changing world. And to do this, we used the Base Outcome Action *(BOA)* process.

An Introduction to Base Outcome Action (BOA)

The starting point in creating a Useful Shift is to identify what's useful. This is the first useful application of the Base outcome Action *(BOA)* process.

1. Where am I? *(Base)*
2. Where do I want to be? *(Outcome)*
3. How do I get there? *(Action)*

The BOA process constricts thinking *(pun intended!)*. It directs our attention to where it needs to be.

It's also highly flexible, and can be wrapped around any situation, at any time!

That's why I suggest using this process whenever you feel like things are getting out of control, in big ways or small.

By shutting all else out, the BOA process helps us to have a laser-like focus on what matters and creates the framework for identifying *(at first)* what is useful.

***

When we're in the midst of a crisis, being disoriented in a storm that engulfs us, it's hard to know where one part begins or ends. Every piece gets jumbled together and it's hard to get our bearings.

The first phase of the BOA process - Base: Where am I? - helped Abbie to get a better sense of what was happening around her.

For Abbie, the crisis was having impacts on what I call the six Elements of Life:

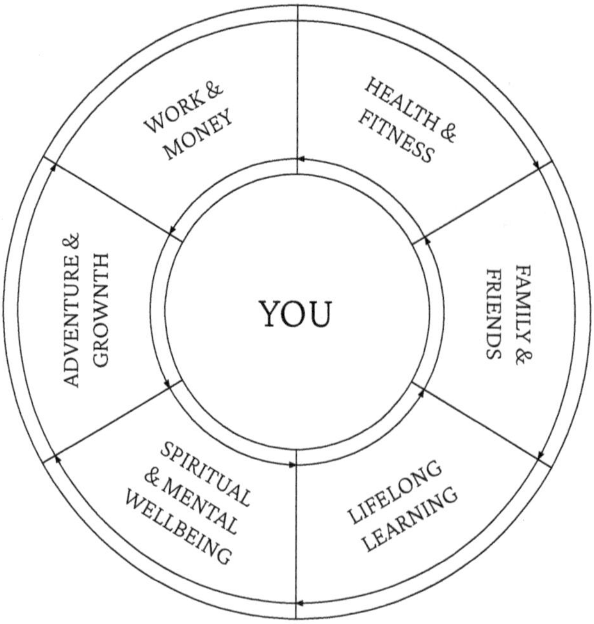

Figure 6: The Six Elements of Life

1. Health and Fitness
2. Family and Friends
3. Lifelong Learning
4. Spiritual & Mental Wellbeing
5. Adventure & Growth
6. Work & Money

For each of the six Elements of Life above, Abbie explored:

- Where am I now?
- What issues am I facing?
- What opportunities do I have?

As we worked through the BOA process together, Abbie was able to cautiously show herself kindness and compassion.

Instead of tumbling and tangling in her tsunami of crisis, Abbie was able to regain her sense of direction, focus, and control.

From there, Abbie was once again able to discern what was useful - and move from self-criticism to self-acceptance and compassion.

Shift

One of the most exciting parts of working with leaders is getting to see how their personal shifts then go on to create organisational shifts. And Abbie was on the cusp of her own.

To me, the word *"shift"* has a profound sense of weight and momentum, and a deliberate effort taking place.

When Dr Martin Luther King Jr. spoke about how *"We must rapidly begin the shift from a 'thing-oriented' society to a 'person-oriented' society,"* he could have used the word transition or change or evolution or pivot. Instead, he chose the word *"shift"*. To truly shift means to have once been in one place, but to have gone to another - not in an incremental way, but in a definitive *"we once were, but now we are"* sense.

A crisis might change us, shake us, move us, affect us, or even destroy us. But it can never shift us. A shift also requires deliberate and concerted effort.

So together, when we speak about creating a Useful Shift, we're speaking about a deliberate, pragmatic, beneficial move from something old to something that serves us in new and more practical ways.

For Abbie, the next part of the BOA process - Outcome - would bring into focus the Useful Shift she needed to take.

Having already looked at her Base *(Where am I?)*, Abbie was once again able to discern what was useful.

From this place of kindness and compassionate acceptance, we were able to explore the next piece of the BOA process - Outcome: *Where do I want to be?:*

- Where do I want to be?
- How do I get there?
- What is the outcome?

In Abbie's case we recognised each life element and worked through each one separately *(Health and Fitness; Family and Friends; Lifelong Learning; Spiritual & Mental Wellbeing; Adventure & Growth; Work & Money).*

Looking at each element separately allowed Abbie the space to see how much was going on in her life. To give herself a break due to the layers of complexity she faced, driven by both internal and external forces. Abbie showed herself some kindness and forgiveness. Acceptance that she was wonderfully human. Both beautiful and broken.

Soon, Abbie had a clear set of pragmatic and valuable Useful Shifts that could serve her, and her organisation, in this time of crisis.

One Thing

With a roadmap of Useful Shifts in front of her, Abbie might have been tempted to take action to implement everything right away.

However, there's one important step left in the BOA Process left - Action: How do I get there?

It's too easy for us to be caught in complexity and the desire to fix it all, now - whether that's in our roles as leaders in the workplace, or in our own personal lives.

But there's one question we should all ask before setting out on a course of action:

'What's the one thing I should be doing right now?'

Amongst all the noise and complexity leader's face, what is the one thing, the most important, impactful and useful thing they can do right now to enable themselves, their team and their business to move forward?

It's an incredibly useful question because it forces us to focus on the most crucial decisions, the decisions that matter above all else. Decisions that will materially impact us and our space, and create the shifts needed to occur.

This is not about limiting ourselves to a single opportunity. Rather, it's about focussing your energy and ability to create a Useful Shift.

In their book The One Thing, Gary Keller and Jay Papasan discuss how a singular focus has a domino effect: *"When one thing, the right thing, is set in motion it can topple many things."*

This is how Abbie created her Useful Shifts, beginning with one particularly useful domino, and building momentum as each shift pushed on the next, through Health and Fitness; Family and Friends; Lifelong Learning; Spiritual & Mental Wellbeing; Adventure & Growth; and Work & Money.

When they didn't fall as expected, Abbie was able to return to the BOA Process and review her Base, identify her Outcomes, and refocus her Action.

Soon, Useful Shifts that began with Abbie were flowing through her team, her projects, her organisation, and having a wider and more meaningful *(dare I say more "useful")* impact than before Abbie's crises.

When COVID-19 hit, I reached out to Abbie to ask how she was coping in this crisis.

She wasn't cocooned from the impact of this new and unexpected global crisis. Like all leaders, the crisis had shaken many of the strategies Abbie had implemented in both her personal and professional life.

However, the BOA Process had stood the test of time - and had given Abbie the pragmatic resilience to lead at a time when leaders were being asked to do more than ever, and to step up where others had faltered or fallen.

I hung up the phone and smiled.

It had indeed been a Useful Shift.

Summary:

Crisis is a constant. Leaders need to be able to navigate crises effectively.

Usefulness helps us to see possibilities, while also helping us to discern the helpful from the unhelpful.

A focus on the One Thing that is most useful right now helps us to focus our effectiveness and create Useful Shifts.

Questions:

In any one of the 6 Elements of Life (*Health and Fitness; Family and Friends; Lifelong Learning; Spiritual & Mental Wellbeing; Adventure & Growth; and Work & Money*), ask:

1. What issues am I facing here?
2. What opportunities do I have here?
3. Where do I want to be?
4. How might I get there?
5. What is the one action I should take right now?

Once you have decided on the One Thing, don't fuss or overthink, Take Action!

About the Author:

Andrew Deering

Andrew Deering is obsessed with helping leaders create a shift into being a better version of themselves. He understands that leaders need to make sense of, and evolve with, the ever-changing complexity businesses face. He does his work by holding the space for the leaders and teams he works with: supporting them on their journey to grow into the potential and possibilities they each have, individually and collectively. He knows that when leaders focus on doing and being better, people and organisations thrive and prosper.

Andrew is known as an expert in building capability through one-on-one coaching, team facilitation, and organisation-wide initiatives. He has spent more than 20 years working with organisations and leaders delivering operational and organisational development and change programs. Andrew has worked with renowned organisations including Shell, the West Australian Government, and Santos. He is also the CEO of The Deering Group, one of Australia's leading experts in organisational transformational capability and change.

His approach of holding the space for others is done through a unique blend of humanity, humility, authenticity and kindness. This allows your people to create the shift they need in a way that enables accelerated outcomes in a safe space.

Act II: Transformation

The Descent

Now that the hero has made a life-changing decision, she has to face the changes that come with it.

CHAPTER SIX

Legacy

Brent Hodgson

Much is written about leadership, culture, organisational development and capability with a future focus - what we can do, what we might change. But so much of it has been written with an ignorance or even disregard for where we have come from - and the powerful influence that legacy has on even the smallest decisions within an organisation, or indeed any collective of people.

A legacy is a complicated concept inside organisations.

We might talk about leaving a legacy, a final lasting monument to our successes for future generations. We might have disdain for legacy, like how we might think about legacy IT systems: old, outdated, redundant, relics of the past that no longer serve us in the present. Or, we might embrace the legacy we've inherited, a good reputation, practice, technique, or culture that contributes to our ongoing success.

We face every crisis carrying the burden, or the benefit, of our legacy.

It tells us the story of the decisions made that led us to be in our current predicament in a moment of crisis.

It's our organisational capability, the tools in our tool belt that we can use to solve the unique problems each crisis presents.

It's the yardstick of preparedness we need to measure up to in order to weather a crisis. Will we be sufficient to rise to the occasion? Or will we fall mercy to the forces that the crisis will inflict on us?

It's valid to want to look backwards at our legacy and achievements and ensure that the good from the past is carried into the future. And then to consider the positive change that you can leave behind through your work.

However, when a crisis is changing the nature of our work, our decisions, our capabilities and our industries, we need to work out how to bring the good from the past into the future. To use our legacy to conquer the crisis.

Because the legacy that got us here will either be our saviour, or our undoing.

Legacies are a powerful force

Consider a lioness teaching her cub to hunt, a bird protecting her chicks from a much larger predator, or the way a person's priorities change after having a baby. Animals and humans alike are evolutionarily hard-wired with the desire to pass on what we've learned, shape the path for those who will take our place, and leave a legacy behind.

Behaviours that are hard-wired into our brains do not simply switch themselves off when we're in a workplace. The legacy motivator permeates our work cultures too. Ask any senior leader in the final decade of their career, and they'll talk about the legacy that they're hoping to leave behind.

On the other side of a legacy, we also do well when we utilise a legacy that has already been created for us.

Another hard-wired behaviour we have is the desire to avoid wasting energy wherever possible. Decision making burns a particularly large amount of our energy. The human brain accounts for around 2% of our weight but uses 20% of our energy. So to manage energy expenditure, we've become adept at finding mental shortcuts.

What a legacy does is give us a shared and historical framework for what we do, and how we do it. It's why we hear things like *"That's not the way we do things around here"*, and *"That doesn't fit our values"*. It's also echoed in slogans like *"The IBM Way"*, *"Quality never goes out of style"*, and *"All the news that's fit to print"*.

This legacy framework comes to drive our work and decision-making. It helps to define the work we do: the assets we decide to invest in, the people we hire, the culture we create, and the policies, systems and procedures that our day-to-day work is built on.

Legacies are mutable

Japan has more than 33,000 businesses known as *"shinise"* - companies that are over 100 years old. These companies have survived wars, famines, floods, tsunamis, earthquakes, political and social upheaval, economic downturns, the rise of competitors and new product innovations, and the complications of intergenerational succession. Yet, in times of turbulence, these companies didn't become irrelevant, stuck in old thinking, with old habits, and dying ways.

One example of this is Hosoo. This 330-year-old company has a proud history manufacturing kimonos, but in recent times, kimono companies struggled to remain profitable as Japanese women opt for more modern, western-style garments.

How does a company like Hosoo remain relevant in a changing world, and remain profitable for the next 300 years?

Masataka Hosoo *(the 12th generation head of the company)* moved Hosoo's focus into carbon fibre manufacturing. This type of precision manufacturing employs many of the same legacy 3D weaving competencies Hosoo mastered over the past 330 years in the production of silk kimonos. It's the kind of unique pedigree that no other manufacturer of carbon fibre could ever dream to boast, particularly since it's one that the organisation was developing almost three centuries before carbon fibre was invented!

Legacy is a zone of core competency that we can use as a base to adapt from.

Legacies are forged in fire

It's easy to assume that legacies are built like the pyramids - as vast monuments, built brick-by-brick in good times.

Rather, they're more likely to be built like trenches - suddenly, and in times of crisis.

Just as Hosoo existed long before the development of carbon fibre parts, Nokia has a corporate history that predates the mobile phones they are best known for today. And both organisations made significant changes to their business models in the midst of crises. Although some of the lustre of the Nokia brand has faded in recent years *(for reasons I'll go into in a moment)*, Nokia's sudden rise from unknown to global powerhouse was fuelled by a particularly painful set of circumstances.

It was the sudden collapse of a major export market *(the Soviet bloc)*, the worst recession Finland had seen in living memory, plus a plummeting stock price providing a triple-crisis, that forced Nokia to adapt - fast!

A new CEO saw the rising potential in the mobile market, and convinced the board to re-engineer the entire organisation from an industrial conglomerate with a history in paper pulp and wires, to a mobile telecommunications centred business.

This helped Nokia go from a loss in 1991, to $1 billion in profit in 1995, to nearly $4 billion in profits by 1999 - and move from an unknown regional industrial company to the 5th most valuable brand in the world, alongside Microsoft, McDonald's, Disney and Google.

It was an incredible leap to fortune, from local manufacturer to global powerhouse. However, it was an opportunity Nokia almost missed.

Prior to this, Nokia's board had dismissed mobile telephony as worthless playthings: *"James Bond gadgets: improbably futuristic and niche devices."*

The triple-crisis Nokia faced gave it the push it needed to build on its core competencies in the way it needed to, to be ready for the boom that lay ahead.

Legacies are for everyone, not just for leaders

Everyone has a hand in shaping an organisation's legacy.

Many of the innovations and changes that grew Nokia into an electronics empire came from individual engineers, not senior executives.

Much of the credit for Nokia's mobile phone success can be traced back to Juha Rapelin, a 32-year-old integrated circuits designer who had a major role in the development of Nokia's first commercially successful mobile phone, the Mobira Cityman.

But it's not just through new technology innovation and new business units that individuals provide organisations with opportunities to build upon their legacy. We also build our organisational legacy through the cultures we create. To borrow a phrase Lieutenant General David Morrison popularised in his 2016 Australian of the Year acceptance speech,

> “*The standard you walk past is the standard you accept*”.

Everyone in an organisation has a hand in creating and shaping an organisation's legacy.

But beware: legacies are a double-edged sword

In a time of crisis, a legacy can be our saviour or our undoing.

In Nokia's case, it was both. Legacy led to its renewal and ascension, and subsequently to its downfall.

The triple-crisis of the early '90s provided Nokia with the push to quickly refocus as a mobile communications company, and eventually emerge as one of the top five brands in the world.

By 2010, Nokia had solidified its position as the leader of mobile phone technology. It had developed the world's most popular smartphone operating system, Symbian OS, a decade ahead of Apple's iOS and Google's Android platforms. All signs suggested Nokia would be in the box seat to capture mass market share of the emerging smartphone market over the years ahead.

But history tells us this didn't happen.

Within three years, Nokia went from one of the world's most valuable brands to liquidating its near-worthless mobile phone assets.

How could an innovative, market-leading company get things so wrong?

Researchers point to Nokia's legacy.

Outwardly, Nokia espoused values of speed and flexibility of decision-making in an agile, well-connected and flat organisational structure. But inside Nokia, one former engineer described it as *"a Soviet bureaucracy"*, where his team had submitted 500 innovation proposals and had zero accepted.

Former Nokia chairman, Risto Siilasmaa, suggests egos had become so swollen after the wildly successful turnaround of the 1990s that a culture of complacency took over the culture of agility and innovation. *(After all, it can be particularly hard to let go of a legacy if that legacy has saved you in the past.)*

Peter Drucker wrote *"The greatest danger in times of turbulence is not the turbulence; it is to act with yesterday's logic."*

The risk of legacy is that it can sometimes be at odds with what we need to do in times of crisis - and cause us to act too slowly, sway us towards decisions that don't serve us, and provide false comfort in the face of crisis.

It took three years of crisis *(1992 to 1995)* for Nokia to reengineer itself from a loss-making industrial to a high-tech and high-profit mobile telephony provider.

Then, it took three years of crisis *(2010 to 2013)* for Nokia to go from the world's leading smartphone brand to liquidating its entire loss-making mobile phone division.

In one crisis, the company rose to the challenge - and built on its legacy.

In the other, the company fell victim to the crisis - and hid within legacy's walls.

How to handle a legacy in a crisis

In the wake of the 2008 Global Financial Crisis, three academics *(Gulati, Nohria and Wohlgezogen)* conducted a study of 4,700 organisations, and the defining strategies that helped some of them roar out of recessions.

Their findings, published in the March 2010 Harvard Business Review article *"Roaring out of Recession"*[1] revealed:

- 80% of organisations surveyed were no longer growing at their pre-crisis levels three years after the crisis.

1 Gulati, R., Nohria, N. and Wohlgezogen, F., 2010. Roaring out of Recession. Harvard Business Review, [online] (March 2010). Available at: <http://firstpersonadvertising.com/wp-content/uploads/Harvard-Business-Review-Roaring-Out-of-a-Recession.pdf>.

- Of those organisations, half were so battered by the crisis that they still hadn't returned to their pre-crisis outcomes three years on.
- And nearly a quarter of them did not survive the recession. They went bankrupt, were liquidated, or unlisted.

Only around 9% of the companies studied were able to thrive after *(and often during)* the crisis, outperforming their competitors by at least 10% in the process.

Companies who employed rush-to-preserve, cut-and-burn, OR grow-while-the-market's-down strategies tended to struggle to perform in the wake of a crisis. But companies who took a deliberate and measured approach to ALL three of the strategies listed below tended to outperform their competitors. In a sense, they worked to build on the strengths that their legacies afforded them.

The three-step process for achieving this is to:

1. Assess.

2. Adapt.

3. Ascend.

Assess

As a starting point, we need to assess where we have come from - not just what is happening around us - and what we would like to do to respond to the crisis around us.

We meet crises while carrying our legacies: the decisions we've made in the past, the histories that we've told, the assets we decided to invest in, the people we've hired, the culture we've created, and the policies, systems and procedures that our work is built on.

Not all of these aspects of a legacy *(as they stand)* will serve us during or after a crisis, and give us the outcomes we hope to achieve.

A starting point for reviewing what parts of your legacy may be useful in the future is to look at the outcomes you want to achieve. Perhaps it's outcomes around revenues and profits. Perhaps it's around organisational capability or impact. Perhaps it's around size or scale. Perhaps it's around stability and resilience.

From there, consider different aspects of your organisational legacy - decisions made, cultures created, people, policies, procedures, systems - and where they fit:

- ***Now*** - What do we have/do/know that serves us now?
- ***Not*** - What old needs do we no longer have, and as a result, what old haves/actions/knowledge will we no longer need?
- ***Next*** - What do we have/do/know that could serve us tomorrow?
- ***Need*** - What do we have/do/know today will be insufficient tomorrow?

Adapt

Organisational change is difficult, and massive legacy leaps are rare. Successful organisational change tends to happen as a series of small, incrementally improving steps rather than through revolutionary changes. Nokia was founded as a paper mill, and became a leading mobile phone brand. But this transformation wasn't through revolution - but rather evolution. It took a series of tiny evolutionary steps over 120 years. In the same way, consider how you can build-on and adapt your existing legacy to respond to the crisis, rather than beginning everything anew.

Ask: *"What is the smallest step we can make to build on our legacy here in order to help achieve our outcome?"*

In the US recession of the early 2000's, office supplies store Staples met the challenge of the crisis by adapting several aspects of their legacy. Here is a summary of their strategy:

- *Now* - Firstly, they recognised that their core business model was still fundamentally as good now as it was previously. The crisis hadn't affected people's need for office supplies.
- *Not* - They closed unprofitable stores that served markets that were not performing.
- *Next* - They identified the value of opening stores in other areas that were more profitable than the stores they closed. The downturn had made the kind of large, prime real estate cheaper Staples' business model relies on cheaper and more abundant - meaning Staples could expand now for less. They also identified new high tech product lines that could bring in new customers and profits!
- *Need* - But these new higher-tech product lines required more in-person sales support in stores. This, combined with the opening of new stores, led Staples to increase the size of their workforce by 10% in the middle of a recession.

As a result of these measures, Staples emerged from the recession stronger than they entered, and over the three years that followed experienced twice the profit growth of their nearest competitor, Office Depot.

Ascend

Where Adapt is all about stepping out, Ascend is all about stepping up and improving the outcomes of all aspects of legacy.

Returning to the 4,700 organisations in the Harvard recession recovery study, businesses that emerged from crisis strongest didn't just continue business as usual.

Instead, they sought opportunities to improve the nature of their work in light of the *"new normal"*.

Yes, they recognised that old assets and people may no longer serve their strategic future, and that cost-cutting might be necessary to ensure otherwise healthy parts of the organisation survive a downturn. But, simultaneously, they understood that investment and innovation are also required in order to emerge stronger after a crisis.

These organisations focussed less on slashing employee numbers, and more on operational efficiencies. They developed new business opportunities, sought additional market share, and created additional production capability.

Operational efficiencies have the dual benefit of improving capability and maintaining morale, as opposed to a cost-cutting *"who's next to be fired"* strategy, which the data suggests has a strongly negative impact on performance over the medium term.

The way you build upon your organisational legacy won't just help you to weather the current crisis, it will also adapt your organisation to be prepared for the next crisis that will inevitably come.

Summary:

When facing a crisis, know what you need to achieve, and Assess your legacy for how it can help or hinder you.

Adapt what you did well into what will serve you well in the future by tweaking your legacy.

Organisations that Ascend well out of crises both cut where needed and improve what remains, with a particular focus around improving revenue generation.

Questions:

1. THEN - In the past, what have we had/done/known that has served us well?
2. NOW - What do we have/do/know that serves us now? *(How do we ascend the value of this?)*
3. NOT - What old needs do we no longer have, and as a result, what old haves/dones/knowns will we no longer need? *(How can we strategically remove these?)*
4. NEXT - What do we have/do/know that could serve us tomorrow? *(How do we tweak and adapt what we already have to fill these gaps?)*
5. NEED - What do we have/do/know today will be insufficient tomorrow? *(How do we tweak and adapt what we already have to fill these gaps?)*

About the Author:

Brent Hodgson

Brent Hodgson is passionately driven by performance, and understanding the tiny differences that make some strategies perform where others falter and fail.

As a speaker, facilitator and strategic coach, Brent helps leaders of purpose-driven businesses to grow and improve profits rapidly. His data-driven approach takes your existing business engine and supercharges the bits that matter most.

With over 20 years working with highly technical organisations in highly competitive industries *(including real estate, investment, telecommunications, software, and business consulting)*, and as the author of 'Unassailable: The Tiny Tweaks that Create an Unbeatable Advantage in Your Marketing' and 'Beyond The Booth: Trade Show Tactics For When Sales Matter', Brent draws on a uniquely diverse set of experiences and studies to support his work.

To find out more about Brent, or to connect directly, visit: www.BrentHodgson.com

CHAPTER SEVEN

Support

Mark Butler

Like most men, I've often shied away from asking for help when I needed it, especially if the support is for something society thinks I 'should' be able to do. Such a reluctance amongst men to seek help for traditionally masculine tasks is so common that there are countless memes and pop-culture references to it - the quintessential examples include asking for directions, lifting something heavy, and changing a tyre.

When I lived in Ireland, the AA *(Automobile Association)* was a roadside vehicle-recovery service. On one of the rare occasions I did ask for help I had no choice - I was in the rain on the side of a highway, with a flat tyre, and without the correct tools to change the tyre myself. Striking up a conversation with the AA guy who came to rescue me, I asked him if they were all mechanics. He told me that they weren't, it wasn't necessary for everyone to be a mechanic, but they all knew enough to get a car started or towed.

Fast forward some years later to Australia, and there was a similar incident. I called the NRMA *(National Roads and Motorists' Association)* as the car I was driving was missing a jack. The representative arrived, and I immediately felt a withering glare from him. I was a young, strong and fit lad and he clearly judged me more than capable of changing a tyre - or, at the very least, having the common sense to have a jack in the car! He went to work and, in the strained atmosphere, I tried to strike up a conversation with him much like my enjoyable conversation years earlier in Ireland, I asked him: *"Are the NRMA guys all mechanics?"* Without even looking up at me, he sneered *"No. We're all f@*king pastry chefs!"*

I laugh about it now but I can recall the feeling of being belittled, judged and made to feel 'less than'. It was enough to make me retreat from the conversation and seek the safety of the driver's seat. I needed help and 'didn't have the tools'. I reached out for help, and was scorned for it.

When people need help and support - whether on the roadside, in a community or in the workplace, it takes a lot to take that step to reach out. Perhaps they don't have the tools or the knowledge to deal with a challenging situation, or perhaps they are unable to help themselves. When people reach out for help and support, they're vulnerable yet courageous, and our response in that moment can make all the difference.

Over the years as a clinical psychotherapist, I have worked with many individuals and groups - veterans, emergency service workers, corporate executives, academics, healthcare professionals, and tradespeople. Mental ill-health does not discriminate, it affects people from all walks of life. The underlying factor that interferes with early recovery is that people are reluctant or scared to come forward. Many people discriminate, hold prejudices, fear and judge people for their issues. Some assume that mental health issues are somehow the fault of the individual, or that they are dangerous and unpredictable. Others don't know what to say to someone suffering, so they say nothing at all, or something unhelpful.

The environment we create is a huge determinant of whether there is enough psychological safety to allow for people to reach out. If their courage and vulnerability are not met with a level of care, or they are scorned or judged as not being 'up to the task'. The ramifications can be devastating. An unhelpful word or changing the subject *(or whatever other defence mechanism someone has to avoid difficult conversations)* can really set a person back. They may never risk reaching out again, at work or anywhere else.

Sometimes, much like changing a tyre, people don't have the 'tools for the job' when they are needed. They may be under duress or distress and feeling like they cannot get the job done. What we are facing in returning to work post-COVID-19 lockdowns will be one of those times for many.

As we emerge back into the sunlight and in most cases return to our traditional workplace, we will experience dramatic shifts in the way people think, cope, relate, communicate and work. We are already starting to see people return to corporate offices with reduced capacity; hybrid environments where some employees continue to work from home while others are in the office, and staggered days to attend the office. Physical changes to the environment such as one-person elevator capacity; canteens, kitchens and coffee machines shut down; desks moved apart; and alternating desks.

Employees and teams will be returning to their workplaces in a different mindset to when the COVID-19 lockdowns began. Many will return to work *(either remotely or physically)* in varying degrees of anxiety, excitement, distress, worry or depression, or some combination of these.

Whilst these physical environmental changes help to protect physical health and are admirable and necessary, organisations have an additional opportunity and responsibility to create an environment that also supports mental health, at this time of deep uncertainty and anxiety.

Post COVID19, one in three of people will be living with or struggling through severe mental distress, according to Monash University research *(2020)*.[1]

In addition to newer cases, those who were already living with mental health problems may have seen those problems become exacerbated, or may have developed a secondary condition. In mental health, one of the more common co-occurring issues is that of depression and anxiety. Estimates show that 60-80% of those with anxiety will show symptoms of depression, and the numbers are similar for those with depression also experiencing anxiety *(Salcedo, 2018[2], Tiller, 2013[3])*. Indeed, the prevalence of people experiencing

---

1 Patty, A., 2020. Employers prepare for return of mentally fragile workforce. Sydney Morning Herald, [online] Available at: <https://www.smh.com.au/business/workplace/employers-prepare-for-return-of-mentally-fragile-workforce-20200521-p54v3o.html> [Accessed 9 August 2020].

2 Salcedo, B., 2018. The Comorbidity of Anxiety and Depression, NAMI. https://www.nami.org/Blogs/NAMI-Blog/January-2018/The-Comorbidity-of-Anxiety-and-Depression

3 Tiller, J., 2012. Depression and anxiety. The Medical Journal of Australia, 1(4), pp.28-31.

more than one condition is only now being more fully understood. During their research in 2018, psychiatrist Oleguer Plana-Ripoll and colleagues discovered that *"every single mental disorder predisposed the patient to every other mental disorder — no matter how distinct the symptoms".* [4] Untreated anxiety and panic disorder can raise the potential for more serious conditions including depression, drug abuse, and suicide. [5]

Leaders will need to lead differently, with different capabilities

Managers and leaders need to approach mental health in their workplace and teams with a new perspective. Regardless of whether the employee is at home, in the office or working flexibly, the legal requirement to provide a safe work environment remains [6]. If an employee could be reasonably deemed to be 'turning up for work' unwell, there lies a duty of care on the organisation to respond to that. This obligation covers not only an environment that is safe for physical health, but one that is safe for mental health. While the overall safe work insurance claims for work-related mental health

4 Plana-Ripoll, O., Pedersen, C., Holtz, Y., Benros, M., Dalsgaard, S., de Jonge, P., Fan, C., Degenhardt, L., Ganna, A., Greve, A., Gunn, J., Iburg, K., Kessing, L., Lee, B., Lim, C., Mors, O., Nordentoft, M., Prior, A., Roest, A., Saha, S., Schork, A., Scott, J., Scott, K., Stedman, T., Sørensen, H., Werge, T., Whiteford, H., Laursen, T., Agerbo, E., Kessler, R., Mortensen, P. and McGrath, J., 2019. Exploring Comorbidity Within Mental Disorders Among a Danish National Population. JAMA Psychiatry, 76(3), pp.259-270.

5 Espey, M., 2020. Can Anxiety and Panic Disorder Cause Depression if Left Untreated?. [Blog] PsychCentral, Available at: <https://psychcentral.com/blog/can-anxiety-and-panic-disorder-cause-depression-if-left-untreated/> [Accessed 9 August 2020].

6 Safe Work Australia. 2020. Working From Home. [online] Available at: <https://www.safeworkaustralia.gov.au/covid-19-information-workplaces/industry-information/general-industry-information/working-home> [Accessed 9 August 2020].

are lower than those for physical injury, they are 2.5 times more expensive, and three times more prolonged on average.[7]

Employees are under no obligation to disclose or divulge their health issues to the organisation despite the employers legal responsibility to create a safe work environment, so it falls on leaders to act to ensure that the environment created is one that promotes wellbeing and positive mental health.

Creating and maintaining such an environment requires a skill-set that many managers and leaders don't possess. In the past, it has been a more comfortable option to direct employees to their Employee Assistance Program[8] or to their Human Resources department to access some support. Yet, often issues with wellbeing and mental health can be quite advanced before those avenues are sought, akin to the ambulance at the bottom of the cliff. Managers and leaders may be asking:

'What do I do if a team member is displaying symptoms of mental illness but they have not told me about any issues?'

'What do I do about performance concerns for team members, including those with mental health problems?'

'I tried to check-in with him a couple of times and he said he was fine.... What more could I have done?'

---

7 Safe Work Australia. 2020. Mental Health. [online] Available at: <https://www.safeworkaustralia.gov.au/topic/mental-health> [Accessed 9 August 2020].

8 A confidential, employer-paid counselling service

'How do I talk about mental health with my colleagues/team?'

'What are my responsibilities when a team member hasn't disclosed their mental illness?'

Normalising the conversation about mental health goes a long way to people feeling that they're able to ask for help when it's needed, and to not feel stigmatised when seeking support.

STIGMA

People fear disclosing their struggle with mindset or mental health problems because of what others will think of them. This fear or anxiety is what stigma, or more particularly self-stigma, looks like.

The anxiety and fear of being judged as somehow being less than their best, letting the side down, not being seen as a team player, not at the top of their game, or maybe not reliable, is enough to cause a person to remain silent and keep it a secret. They continue to 'tough it out' and come to work. This internalised fear of what people might think leads us to take-on what we perceive to be the judgement of others.

Stigma is a social construct. Mental health doesn't cause stigma, people do. As Daniel S Goldberg, an expert on stigma, says, *"it is always people who stigmatise other people"*[9]. Whether someone is actually stigmatised or not, if they feel or imagine it then the result is the same. This is known as self-stigma. If the stigma is imposed

9 Goldberg, D.S. 2017. On Stigma & Health. The Journal of Law, Medicine & Ethics, 45(4): 475-83.

by others, rather than being self-perceived, it will manifest from a prejudice and usually results in discriminatory behaviour.

Regardless of whether stigma of mental health is imposed or perceived, the solution is to inform and educate leaders in an organisation in what to look for in mental health issues and how they manifest , and what steps to take to get in front of potential issues and ultimately support those who need it.

Daniel Goleman says in his book *"Emotional Intelligence'* - *"The most powerful form of non-defensive listening, of course, is empathy: actually hearing the feelings behind what is being said."* Emotional Intelligence *(EQ)* and empathy are increasingly becoming essential skills that are needed to get out in front of mental health issues before they take hold. Organisations need to get ahead of the curve, rather than to flatten the curve, to use more recent language.

There is always a solid case to be made for developing self-awareness and the awareness of others, as well as resilience training programs, mindfulness and healthy living sessions. These supports help develop the resilience of teams and assist in tackling stress in the workplace. However, they can be a bit 'one-size-fits-all', rather than addressing the complexity involved in mental health, and realising that different people have differing needs at different times. We need to be able to have a meaningful conversation with anyone and 'meet them wherever they are at' on the scale of distress or support they distinctively need. This requires levels of empathy and EQ to be developed, which are necessary skills for leaders today.

Breaking Down the Stigma

It's increasingly important that organisations are able to create an environment that builds awareness of mental health, safeguard mental wellbeing, and tackle and reduce stigma. There are three main methods that can be deployed:

Public campaigns: Public campaigns such as RUOK Day can be effective in raising awareness, if the effort is sustained and supported with additional education. Whilst an event like RUOK Day can provide the opportunity for individuals to feel safe opening up a conversation about their mental health, people are not always equipped with the tools to handle that conversation in a supportive way, should it arise. These additional tools and resources are necessary so that people who need help can feel supported.

Mental Health First Aid: Mental Health First Aid training is valuable to a business. However the training sometimes comes at a significant time commitment and cost, and so it is often only a few designated mental health first aid officers who have access to the training. Also, the lessons must be re-learned and applied regularly, else the knowledge can dissipate over time. Having a designated mental health first aid officer can provide much needed support when people don't know where else to get help.

Contact-based strategies: Contact-based strategies are the 'holy grail' of a mental health strategy in any organisation, not only destigmatising mental health, but providing the tools to support those who need it. They involve interpersonal conversation, nurturing an environment where real people are discussing real issues and experiences with their peers. Contact-based strategies work best when driven from the top down, where senior people in the organisation can lead by example, sharing their experience of mental health issues, or those of someone close to them. Others in the organisation see that mental health doesn't change the essence of who those leaders are, that they are far more than their diagnoses and that mental health doesn't need to stand in the way of success. This approach is a powerful way of building and sustaining a diverse and inclusive culture, and can become a key plank in wellbeing, leadership, and performance programs within the organisation.

Leaders in organisations can make an impact on the mental wellbeing today that will ripple for years throughout the organisation, changing the lives of their peers and teams in ways that they may never fully realise. If we can become comfortable having conversations around our own experiences with mental health, we can send a powerful cultural signal that normalises conversations about mental health, and removes stigma. If we can be upskilled about what to look for, we might be able to ask the right question at the right time for someone who needs some help. And if we can be comfortable in a conversation around mental health, we can share in another's journey and provide the right support when they are at their most vulnerable.

Beyond the obvious improvement in the health and safety of our people and business, contact-based conversations bring people together, offering team cohesion and mutual support. They are key to creating the optimal environment for success and performance.

As we emerge from this crisis, people will need a supportive mental health environment more than ever before. Those who need help may feel that they're unable to seek it out. They may not have the tools or the know-how to change their situation. We can be ready now to help them change their tyres and get back on the road. We don't need to be a mechanic, just don't tell them you're a *"f*&king pastry chef"*.

> *What mental health needs is more sunlight, more candour, and more unashamed conversation. – Glenn Close*

Summary:

Some people will be unsure, apprehensive, and fearful. They will not want to risk seeking support and exposing themselves to judgement or criticism. It is a natural reaction to feeling unsafe and unsure, but they will continue to present for work (either at home or in the workplace) in a less than ideal state rather than feel judged or take any time off to get better.

If people don't feel safe in seeking support, then we won't know how to support them. This issue is right in front of us, right now. It doesn't discriminate. So, we need to 'Get in Front' and intervene as early as possible. We cannot sit in a glass-bottomed boat, waiting to drift over an issue before responding. The value in investing in early intervention and prevention strategies is well-known and financially sound.

Leaders and managers need to be upskilled in learning the essential skills to help them know what to know, what to look for and what to say and do - empathetically, safely, and early. Developing this skill set helps to develop the leader's own empathy and emotional intelligence. We need to be able to have deep conversations with colleagues about mental health and how we can support someone to safely bring their 'whole selves' to work.

Questions:

1. What can we see in our people?

How are they today? Do they seem engaged? Are they distracted? Are they isolating? Are they being cynical and disruptive?

2. What can we do for them right now?

How can we check in safely with them? How can we help them feel secure and they belong? What do I say?

3. What can we do better?

I need new skills now, how could I best use them? Why did we wait until there were visible signs of distress? Could we have reached out sooner? How can we support the team around this?

About the Author:

Mark Butler

Mark Butler is a mental-health specialist in the areas of anxiety, depression, burnout, trauma, substance use and related issues. With 12 years' clinical psychotherapy experience, underpinned by 25 years' commercial experience, he has earned a reputation for creating the conditions to deliver peak performance.

He helps individuals, teams and organisations to get in front of potential mindset and mental health issues, deal effectively with stress and burnout to optimise resilience, promote growth mindset and fulfil their potential.

Mark holds a Master of Addictive Behaviours, a Master of Gestalt Psychotherapy, Diploma in Gestalt Counselling, is an accredited clinical psychotherapist, a certified resilience coach and with further therapeutic training in Schema Therapy, PTSD treatment, Anxiety Education for Health Professionals, and Recovery Group Facilitation *(Yalom)*.

The Eye of the Storm

in which the hero presses forward despite difficulty, and experiences early success along the journey

CHAPTER EIGHT

Adapt

Lynne Cazaly

Plenty of leaders, businesses and politicians have been spruiking the need for greater agility ... and they've been doing it for years! Agility and adaptability isn't new.

But *how* we change ... now that could be new.

Agility is a cultural and mindset shift thousands of businesses the world over have adopted; it's an approach that's changing the world of work. In recent times of great global change, we've all experienced a need to be more flexible, adaptable and agile.

The Institute for the Future some years ago suggested 2020 would be when capabilities and skills like sensemaking, cognitive load coping and adaptive thinking would be required.

They weren't wrong!

If we just take the capability and performance of ***adaptability – the capability of being able to adjust to changing circumstances*** – and zoom in on that, surely we'll do be able to cope and do well, no matter what the world throws at us.

The call to adapt

We respond to a call for adaptability in different ways.

Something happens – an event – and while we might want the status quo to remain, we aren't going to get it!

Older ways of thinking and working – staying as we are, using older systems, structures and ways of thinking, will ultimately take us towards obsolescence. Business performance will decline and everything will take longer, cost more and be harder to do.

Rather than playing passively and *'waiting to see what happens'*, we can get on the front foot, respond to the change and do something with it.

This is the *'adjusting to changing circumstances'* of adaptability.

Newer ways of thinking and working need us to be tuned in and aware to the changes going on, and being ready and willing to adapt. This helps improve business performance, but it does need a mindset shift to make things happen sooner, quicker, easier.

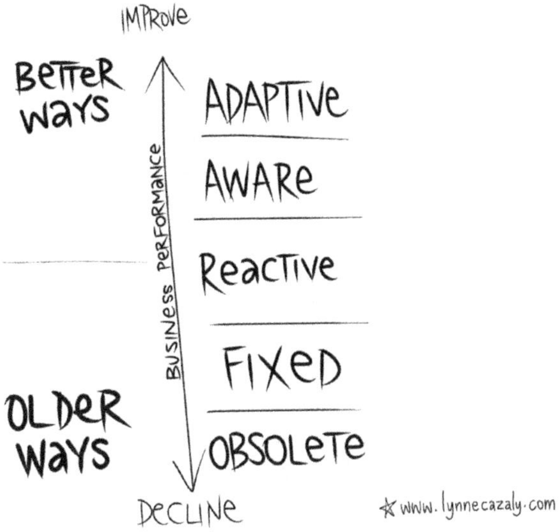

Figure 7: Obsolete to Adaptive

Variations of adaptability

As the effects of the COVID-19 lockdowns and isolations closed up retail outlets in so many cities, I had my eye on several restaurants and cafés in Melbourne, my home-town, watching if they and how they would adapt and change.

Here are just four examples on the variations of adaptability.

1. Many eateries closed their doors, waiting for it all to be over. They were either out of business and gone, or winding things

up for operations as the restrictions eased. Adapting? Yes. Perhaps more like hibernation?

2. A big barn of a café stayed as they were, changing only a bench, dragging it closer to the front door so they could serve customers outside, without them having to go inside. Adapting? Yes. A little.

3. An award-winning eatery sold the products they use when they're making their scrumptious pasta and associated Italian fare. Their 'deli fridge' in the heart of the restaurant was a new experience! Now we could use THE EXACT PRODUCTS they use! It was as if the curtain had been drawn back and we could now see the workings of the orchestra at a live musical theatre or see the magician's swift and subtle moves behind the magic trick. Special ingredients were now available to us. And there we were, bless us, trying to replicate the restaurant menu using the products at home but not quite getting there. Ever hopeful of a quick return to opening their doors, we enjoyed the flavours but something wasn't like the original. But they stayed open, trading, employing staff, trying something different. Adapting? Absolutely.

4. A high-end restaurant decided to close its doors only to open a few weeks later with 'take home packs'. Not a standard take away menu that many shops and eateries continued with, but specific ingredients from their list of menu favourites. The items *(including condiments)* were par-baked, packaged and included clear instructions from the chef on how to cook, bake, and serve. This was getting closer to the real thing! Another level of adaptation on their offering. They had a different theme and each week invited customers to place orders early in the week and then collect them on Saturday mornings. The restaurant kept their supplier chains operating, kitchen staff working and the brand visible, reaching out, deep into the homes of their customers. One of

their packs included branded wine glasses and bottles of wine. Now they're visible and with us every time we say 'Cheers!'

They also opened up their decoration storage gold mine, equivalent to the props supplies used on a film set. Customers were able to buy from their stockpile of decorations, décor and themed objects. Now could have even more of the restaurant in our homes!

These are all examples of unique and tailored adaptations.

They are all adjusting – or not - to the circumstances and responding with the solutions that suit them, that they have decided.

The problem – particularly in agile ways of working – of following the golden child 'Spotify model' *(of the Swedish online music streamer, that lives and breathes an adaptable, every changing agile mindset)* is that it was designed and created by Spotify, for Spotify.

These things aren't as transferrable or able to be overlayed or placed on another unique organisation as we might think. Sure, some of the principles and ideas might apply, but thinking there is a prescription for adaptability negates the whole idea of adaptability.

If you follow what another has followed, are you really adapting or just copying, replicating? It doesn't take your customers, environment, products and services, team members, leadership, culture, economics, solutions and intellectual property into account. It would be foolish change for changes sake, not adaptability to adjust to changing circumstances.

So how do you adapt?

There's no point changing in a vacuum, thinking that what you change won't have an impact on customers and users, stakeholders and teams.

Adaptability starts with getting closer.

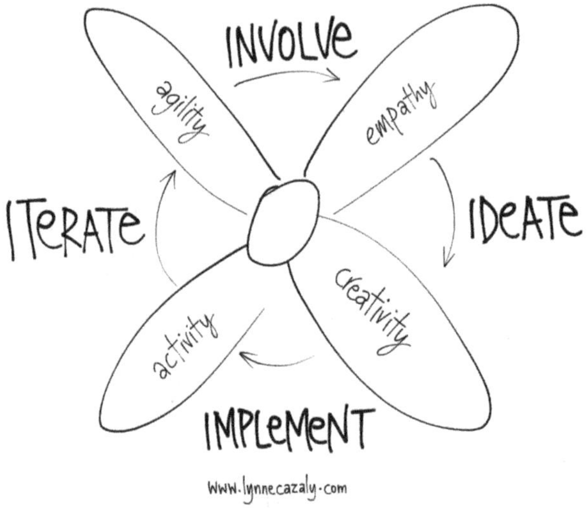

Figure 8

Involve

This is about involving people, users, customers, colleagues. It means connecting more with people, not less. It's being closer to them and understanding more about who they are, what they need, what their problems and challenges are.

It's empathy. Connecting with people, understanding things from their perspective and seeing the truth of the situation or problem. You know you've experienced a lack of empathy from a friend or colleague – or a customer experience – where your view or experience just didn't register. They didn't seem to care or they didn't make you feel like they cared or knew what you were going through. To adapt, we must at first care enough to want to adapt.

Looking at the eateries, the restaurant who shared the popular menu favourites were tuned in to what customers love about them.

Ideate

This is about generating ideas and possibilities, solutions and answers and new ways of working, being and doing. It could be creating a new process or reducing how long the existing one takes.

When a postal provider looked at improving the time it took for a business to create a new online account, they were keen to reduce it from the previous 18 days to something a little quicker! By involving the team, users and customers and other parts of the business, they were able to generate ideas and ways of getting boxes ticked and forms filled out. At the end of their ideation process, they'd been able to reduce that time of creating a new business account down to two days. And that was a few years ago. I'm sure it's almost instantaneous now. Like most of our expectations, we want it now and this postal provider found a host of ideas and ways to make that happen. Without the ideas, the potential for adaptation couldn't have happened.

It's about creativity.

We may not think we're very creative but we're going to need to get over that mindset because we need ingenuity and innovation to generate possibilities in order to adapt. It's more than a clichéd brainstorming session in a dull meeting room. Contemporary creativity research identifies that boredom, daydreaming, walking, talking, reading, thinking and even showering are all good places to get ideas to adapt!

The eateries? Plenty of ideas there: moving the bench in one café, having the deli fridge in another, branded wine glasses and wines – they're all great ideas for adapting what they normally do.

Implement

Now it's time to put the ideas, possibilities and solutions to work, putting them into practice. It's an experimental thing. It won't be perfect. This is where you need to invite and tolerate some failures and learning. Don't put so much pressure on people that they're fearful of implementing things because they know they might not work perfectly. Relax the expectation. This is an experiment, it's a laboratory not a courtroom; let's see what happens.

It's about activity.

There is a point where we need to stop talking or stop planning and put something out there into the world. It's time to print, publish, ship, sell, test... whatever you need to do to spin the wheels on the thing. It can be a scary time because who knows what will happen next. And this is the path to adaptation.

All of the eateries were experimenting with something. Time tells after a number of transactions, customers, days or meals what is worth continuing with and what's worth changing.

Iterate

After a few experiments you'll have some results, responses, answers and information. We can improve, adjust, add a bit here, remove a bit there and go again. We repeat it but with the insights of learning from the implementation.

It's about agility.

Being quick to market is one thing; being quick to market with something that people want, love and use is a whole other thing. The best way to be adaptable is to listen to and look at what happened when you implemented. Then make changes – big and small. Tweak and try it again. Improve and incrementally experiment. Again.

What will the eateries do as the world continues to evolve? Will they continue their home delivered options or 'our restaurant – your place' choices? The tweaks will be visible over time.

In summary, involving and empathy requires a connection. Ask and listen.

Ideas come from thinking. Talk and think.

Implement is a verb. Put something into practice.

And iteration is evolution. Get ready to change. Again.

There is a flow or cycle to being adaptable. I don't see it as overly prescriptive, rather it's suggestive. It's no box or grid that you must follow; it's no matrix that you need to fill the spaces of. It's a flow of ongoing movement and momentum.

By all means spend as long as you like on each stage. You might like to spend the next quarter just working on the first thing; and then tackle the others. Perhaps you'll look at the next thing when the team's ready. Or perhaps in that new role you're aiming for. Maybe it will be a clean start or clean break, a clean slate. Embracing a major adaptation by next Tuesday may be a little high on expectations. You only have to adapt a little at first.

As any leader, team or organisation creating a culture of adaptability will tell you, they are likely on a 'journey'. Hey, who isn't! You might not remember when or where it started or how it started, but it started. They may not be able to show you exactly where they are but they are in some type of change and ongoing adaptation… a ceaseless transformation. And we may never 'get there', it's just the next change, the next adaptation. This is a new way of working indeed.

Summary:

The world is changing and we need to change with it – that's why adaptability is a key capability that we need.

Copying other company's strategies don't give us the opportunity to adapt for our customers and unique situation.

You need only start adapting something small and you'll see what the results are; then you can adapt something else, and keep going.

Questions:

1. How open were you to changes that have recently occurred?
2. Could you have changed even more than you did?
3. What further changes are you now noticing in your industry or sector?
4. How have you seen different businesses change and adapt in recent times?
5. Which parts of your business have now revealed themselves as being stuck, rigid or too slow to adapt?

About the Author:

Lynne Cazaly

Lynne Cazaly helps individuals, teams and organisations transition to better ways of thinking and working. She is an expert in adaptability and sensemaking.

Lynne is an international keynote speaker, author and a master facilitator. She is the author of 6 books: 'ish: The Problem with our Pursuit for Perfection and the Life-Changing Practice of Good Enough', 'Agile-ish: How to Create a Culture of Agility', 'Leader as Facilitator: How to Engage, Inspire and Get Work Done', 'Making Sense: A Handbook for the Future of Work ', 'Create Change: How to Apply Innovation in an Era of Uncertainty', and 'Visual Mojo: How to Capture Thinking, Convey Information and Collaborate Using Visuals'

She works with executives, senior leaders and project teams on their change and transformation projects. This includes working with agile practices, business agility improvements and digital transformations.

Lynne is an experienced radio broadcaster, presenter and producer having presented more than 10000 hours on-air. Her background is as a communication specialist, having lectured in under-graduate and post-graduate programs in several of Australia's Universities and consulting to different industries, sectors and fields on engagement, communication and change.

Lynne can help you think better, make sense of information and handle the realities of information overload with her clever hacks and ingenious processes, tools and methods. She is a cognitive load coping expert.

Lynne is an experienced board director and chair and an #avgeek, loving everything aviation and air traffic control.

CHAPTER NINE

Perform

Alessandra Edwards

As the panic of the pandemic subsides around the globe and organisations slowly tiptoe out of lockdown, leaders will open the door onto a landscape they haven't navigated before. The unspoken threat of further pandemic waves; the uncertainty as to what business may look like in the next 12 months; and the mixed anxiety and excitement about returning to the office. It feels less like an opportunity and more like the beginning of an endurance expedition into unknown territory. Leaders have no compass, no reference points, no known end date to the journey, and an expedition team that has likely emerged from working from home bruised, battered, and exhausted. Not exactly the makings of a successful Indiana Jones adventure.

Leaders are noticing that the COVID-19 crisis has affected their people in very different ways. Some are exhausted and unmotivated. Some are struggling with the negative mental effects triggered by social distancing and working from home. They are hesitant to leave behind the new, slower pace of life in order to head back to the office. Overall, leaders are not feeling confident that their team post-COVID have the stamina, the endurance, and the mental strength necessary for the long journey ahead.

The DNA of Performance

There's a good reason why people *(and indeed organisations)* have responded the way they have. It's a reason that runs deep into our core - into the DNA of performance. And understanding this DNA of performance creates an opportunity to thrive in ways we have never known before.

The term opportunity, which is currently replacing the word 'pivot' as the word du jour, comes from the Latin expression 'ob portum veniens', meaning coming towards a port. It was once a mariner's term used to communicate that the direction of the wind at sea had changed, allowing the most favourable window to steer safely into port. In that context, opportunity meant to deploy every skill of navigation, vision, leadership, and observation in order to reach a known destination safely. Today, we typically use the term to mean making the most of a crisis. Captain and crew already had developed all the skills, the capability and the vision necessary to help them position the ship in the best possible place, so that as soon as the wind changed, they could charge ahead swiftly and safely.

Like captains, leaders cannot control the environment, the weather or the currents but they can control their own ship, and develop their crew's capability and stamina so that everyone can remain in a strong holding pattern, despite the adverse elements, and be ready to deploy quick action when the opportunity arises. Leaders need to have a deep understanding of how well their ship is built and what the inherent weaknesses and strengths are in order to calculate risks and take pre-emptive action.

The work I do with leaders and teams revolves around developing this deep understanding of self-risk through the lens of DNA and genetics.

DNA and genetics underpin every aspect of us, and the way we interact with the world. We can't change our genetic blueprint. Our DNA *(for better or worse)* isn't our fault. But we can negotiate better outcomes from it. By working within the framework your DNA provides, you can reduce risk and enhance performance. Not only does this provide us with a helpful metaphor for how we can respond to opportunities and limitations, it also provides us with practical insights that can apply to us - as individuals, and as collectives within organisations.

Tired or Thriving?

It is no coincidence that some people will emerge from lockdown tired and mentally unfocused, while others are thriving through most of the crisis. This has little to do with COVID-19 and everything to do with our unique genetics. At DNA level, humans are 99.9% the same *(Collins & Mansoura, 2001)*[1]. This means that everyone in your team, including you, is roughly 99.9% identical to their colleagues. It is the 0.1% difference that accounts for the huge variations in the sustainability of energy, stamina, performance, and whether we strive or thrive under stress.

1 Collins, F.S & Mansoura, M.K. 2001. The Human Genome Project Revealing the shared inheritance of all humankind . Cancer. 91(1 Suppl), pp. 221-225.

This is also the reason why many people entered the COVID-19 crisis with their sails already at half-mast. Over the last two decades, the pace of life has been fast and challenging. Many people were struggling under the constant flooding of requests and obligations from work and life, while feeling guilty they were not able to stay on top of things. From reputable publications to social media articles the message was clear: stress is our fault. We should be implementing sleep, exercise and mindset strategies to work smarter not harder; we should turn off our screens at night, eat a healthy diet and aim to exercise at least three times a week, more if we are really aiming for high performance. As people failed to attain this mythical work/life balance, they continued at a frenzied pace, constantly chasing the new email, the new project in a never-ending cycle of catch up and self-disappointment. Most started to ignore the red flags of dysfunction such as exhaustion, insomnia, mood swings, inability to find inner peace and focus while telling themselves this was the new normal. They band-aided exhaustion with caffeine, insomnia with Ambien and emotional turmoil with alcohol or sugar.

The truth is that COVID-19 did not create all of this. It merely amplified the unsustainability of a system that demanded we work and live at a speed that our genes and biology have not had the chance to evolve into. In the same way, COVID-19 didn't create the dysfunctions and challenges our organisations have as they emerge from the coronavirus crisis. It merely brought to light the existing issues of a slowly evolving organisational DNA in the context of a rapidly changing environment.

Biological evolution is very slow – it takes around a million years for evolutionary change to occur. But society and technology evolve fast and so we have seen major changes in our life and environment over the course of just a few decades. The problem is that our DNA has not had the chance to adapt to our modern patterns and behaviours. Our genes are still designed to thrive in an environment where survival is dependent upon regular, intense bouts of exercise, where optimal energy results from cycles of fasting and feasting, where resilience is only sustained when we get to experience extreme but relatively short doses of fear, and where our lives literally depend upon creativity and innovation.

Adapting to a New World

When we decided to embrace the fast, new world of technology and 24/7 connectivity, we had no idea that we were creating an environment that would impact our performance, wellbeing and mental robustness within a couple of decades. Exhaustion, insomnia, depression and anxiety are at an all-time high world-wide[2][3]. A global survey commissioned by Regus of 1,000 corporations across 15 countries worldwide found that 60% of workers in global economies are experiencing more stress today than they did just two years prior[4].

There is also increased evidence that the interplay between our DNA and stress levels have a profound impact on our physical and mental wellbeing[5]. Even temporary high levels of stress can affect a process known as DNA methylation, and result in permanent

2 American psychological association. 2020. Stress in America 2020. [Online]. [15 July 2020]. Available from: https://www.apa.org/news/press/releases/stress/2020/report

3 Australian institute of health and welfare . 2020. Stress and Trauma. [Online]. [1 August 2020]. Available from: https://www.aihw.gov.au/reports/australias-health/stress-and-trauma

4 Dr Judy, E. c2020. Global Organisation for Stress: Stress levels are rising worldwide. [Online]. [15 July 2020]. Available from: http://www.gostress.com/stress-levels-are-rising-worldwide/

5 Powell et al.. 2013. Social stress up-regulates inflammatory gene expression in the leukocyte transcriptome via -adrenergic induction of myelopoiesis. Proceedings of the National Academy of Sciences. 110(41)

changes to the expression and characteristics of genes [6]. These changes can even be epigenetic - causing changes that are then passed down from generation to generation.

This is not our fault. It is simply the result of the growing gap between our environment and our inherited genetic legacy.

As with individuals, organisations may also have a growing gap between their organisational DNA or legacy, and their changing environment. We may not be able to change the organisation's DNA just as much as we cannot change our own DNA, but we can understand it and negotiate with it so as to rig the sails as we head towards future opportunities. Once we understand the specific behaviours that help us develop our own unique strength, it is much easier to make choices and develop habits for sustainable performance. At an organisational level, we can understand where the inherited weakness may lie and make changes that are still congruent at a DNA level but that strengthen the whole system. Strong organisations grow strong leaders, who lead strong teams.

At a biological level, energy, emotions and stress responses are complex chemicals that are built and broken-down following instructions from our genes. We experience these as vitality, mood and resilience but at a cellular level they are the result of the complex interaction between our genes and our environment. While adopting a specific mindset is useful, it is not enough to override our specific DNA tendencies.

Understanding our DNA

6 Glad et al.. 2017. Reduced DNA methylation and psychopathology following endogenous hypercortisolism – a genome-wide study. Scientific Reports. 28(7), pp. 44445.

The starting point in helping individuals to understand their own DNA of performance is to literally map their genetic blueprint. *(This means taking a swab, and sending a sample of their DNA to a lab to be analysed. When this is not possible, a proprietary diagnostic questionnaire is used.)*

I often work with leaders who have two copies of what's become known as the *"CEO gene"*, a dopamine transporter that evokes strong notions of leadership, reward and motivation. This gives them a competitive advantage in terms of being self-motivators, great thinkers, with an active prefrontal cortex that allows them to see clear long-term vision and develop a big picture strategy.

These are generally the people who lead from the front, who have a great ability to motivate self and others. If lockdown allowed them to experience a less frenetic pace, it is likely they're coming out on top, feeling in control, calm and clear headed.

However, the gene that allows these individuals to thrive as leaders also has a dark side. The *"CEO gene"* also makes it harder for these leaders to switch off under pressure. When under high levels of stress, they tend to become frustrated and judgemental of their peers and team, leading them to pile more onto their plate instead of delegating as they feel no one is performing to their standard. As a result, they often suffer from insomnia, difficulty falling asleep at night, mental rumination and often, great anger.

Another gene that can both help or hinder us in these circumstances is the *"Warrior Gene"* - which is involved in the breakdown of neurotransmitters *(serotonin, adrenaline, noradrenaline, and dopamine)* that regulate mood, sleep, appetite and motivation. People with two copies of the Warrior gene tend to be low self-motivators, needing lots of variety in their schedule to activate their prefrontal cortex. However, these people most likely thrived in the initial phases of lockdown. The change from the office routine to working from home would have pushed up their dopamine and noradrenaline levels, giving them focus, excellent cognitive performance and the best energy.

Having a team where the majority of people have two copies of the CEO gene could be problematic in terms of communication and delegation. Tempers could run hot and toxic communication could undermine any efforts to foster psychological safety within the team.

On the other hand, having a team where the majority of people carry the Warrior gene, would also be a challenge as they can struggle with motivation, energy and completing projects on time.

Enduring the long post-peak pandemic Road to Recovery

As we enter the endurance phase of the pandemic, with more uncertainty, less precedent and no idea of the finish line, having a deep understanding of how our genes perform under pressure can help us to thrive. How they can up or down regulate our energy for endurance. How they influence the way we relate and communicate with others gives us a huge competitive advantage as well as a clear blueprint on what we could be focusing on to thrive.

Moving deeper into the era of disruption, leaders need to recognise that organisations and teams are made of people whose quality of performance is in great part genetically driven. We need to abandon the delusion that a one-size-fits-all approach to wellbeing and performance is relevant and effective. The visionary leader who is navigating uncharted waters needs a strong team who can react quickly, recover from the fallout of unpredictable crises, and who have the physical, mental and emotional capability to improvise and innovate on the go. They need to be able to adapt and sustain their strength and performance over long periods of uncertainty and change. It is time to start to build an awareness of the DNA of ourselves and our organisations. Only by doing so can we ensure our teams and the individuals within them are positioned to best utilise their unique strengths, as we set sail for the opportunities that lie ahead.

Summary:

The DNA of Performance model provides practical insight into the environment we navigate in our day-to-day lives, as well as both practical and metaphorical insights into how our organisations function.

Although we can't change our genetic blueprint, we can negotiate better outcomes - responding to the immutable DNA at our core in ways that reduce risks, and enhance performance.

Avoid the delusion of one-size-fits-all approaches. An awareness of your personal (or organisational) DNA allows you to play to strengths, and navigate weaknesses, facing whatever crisis you encounter with courage and stamina.

Questions:

For you and your team:

1. What specific work and lifestyle behaviours increase your performance over time?
2. What specific work and lifestyle behaviours decrease your performance over time?
3. How does pressure affect your communication style?
4. How does pressure affect your motivation?
5. Rate your stamina right now out of 5. Is this below or above where this metric usually sits? Where, ideally, would you like it to be?

About the Author:

Alessandra Edwards

Alessandra Edwards is a peak performance and wellbeing mentor, author and trainer. She has over a decade's experience working at the cutting edge of DNA-based health and ultra-wellness programs for senior leaders and their teams who want to reach their highest level of physical and mental performance.

You can find our more about Alessandra at alessandraedwards.com

All is Lost

In which the hero faces a reversal. The villain is back and she can't understand where everything went wrong. Yet there is hope...

CHAPTER TEN

Plan

Dr Rebecca Sutherns

"Plan? Now?"

When I first began writing this chapter, it was day 26 of COVID-19 cocooning at home. We'd been radically disrupted and shaken to our core. By today, I've lost count. The shock is wearing off but the ride isn't over yet. By the time you read this, our worlds will have changed again and again.

The idea of strategic planning in the middle of a pandemic seems crazy. The pandemic has thrown so many twists and turns at us that it's difficult to know where we'll be next week, let alone next year.

Suddenly our previous plans seem irrelevant, and our ability to predict the future with any certainty seems non-existent. Not to mention the fact that people are busy, distracted, exhausted and hitting what's known as the *"third quarter slump."*[1]

We couldn't have planned for COVID-19's emergence or effects. So how can we plan during it? Should we even try to? Is it wise to do any strategic planning when our future is so uncertain?

If there ever was one key reason to conduct strategic planning, it would be to create momentum. Organizations, like motorcycles, thrive on momentum. A stationary motorcycle is precarious and unsteady, unable to stay upright without being supported. But with momentum, it finds balance and stability.

Likewise, when you ride a motorcycle, staying upright is easier if you're looking in the direction you want to travel. The motorcycle responds positively when you are clear about your intention and your gaze is fixed on the horizon, rather than where you are right now, or only a short distance ahead. In strategy, as in motorcycle riding, we become more likely to topple and fall if we look exclusively to the immediate environment or to the short-term. A longer-term focus on where we want to go, combined with momentum in that direction, creates balance and stability

If you're unsure of the value of strategy in a world that's so uncertain, here are some points to consider:

---

1 See, for example: Purtill, J., 2020. We have begun the dreaded third quarter of isolation, when — yes — things get weird. Triple J Hack, [online] Available at: <https://www.abc.net.au/triplej/programs/hack/coronavirus-covid19-isolation-third-quarter-phenomenon-has-begun/12190270>

1. Strategy is about making choices.

As Peter Drucker said,

> *"The key to strategy is omission."*

People are craving decisive leadership as a counterbalance to widespread uncertainty. Even in times of disruptive change, or perhaps especially now, leaders have choices to make. These choices are primarily about where to put your attention and where not to. Given you are making choices every day, having a strategy in place lets you make them with intentionality and clear reference points.

2. Strategy spurs you into action.

Developing a series of action steps against a timeline is a lever that will help you overcome inertia or the paralysis of overwhelm. Even if those action steps prove to be *"the wrong ones,"* any sailor, athletic coach, or indeed motorcyclist will tell you that it is easier to change direction while you are moving than when you are stationary.

3. Strategy makes you proactive, not reactive.

Having a plan gets you on your front foot and ready for whatever comes, even if that future doesn't match your initial expectations. The sense of agency that accompanies having a plan is a calming and motivating force.

4. Clear strategy is a competitive advantage.

Done well, having a strategy sets you apart. As A.G. Lafley and Roger Martin write in Playing to Win,

> *Not only is strategy possible in times of tumultuous change, but it can be a competitive advantage and a source of significant value creation.* [2]"

Roger Rumelt expresses it like this in Good Strategy/Bad Strategy: no one has an advantage at everything — press where you have it, sidestep where you don't. [3] Taking the time to develop a clear strategy during a time of crisis is an opportunity to press.

5. Strong strategy attracts resources.

Investors want to back people with a compelling vision and a plan for achieving it. Leaders who take initiative and develop compelling strategies for utilizing resources tend to receive the resources they need to execute those strategies. Leaders who do not develop strong strategy tend to find themselves complaining that they have insufficient resources for effective execution.

6. Strategy creates buy-in.

The co-creation of strategy with your team is a learning process that builds understanding, cohesion and buy-in. The power of a shared experience and a co-created product is no less true in times of turbulence than of greater stability.

7. Strategic planning challenges you to lift performance.

---

2 A.G. Lafley & Roger L. Martin, Playing to Win: How Strategy Really Works (Harvard Business Review Press, 2013): 4

3 Richard Rumelt, Good Strategy/Bad Strategy: The Difference and Why It Matters (Profile Books Ltd, 2017)

Football coach Tom Landry famously said,

> "*A coach is someone who tells you what you don't want to hear, who has you see what you don't want to see, so you can be who you have always known you could be.*"

To the extent that you draw on trusted advisors to help your organization develop strategy, the value of those thinking partners' perspectives is particularly high in unpredictable times where our past experiences are not faithful reference points for the future.

8. Times of crisis help you to clarify strategy.

The issues you are experiencing now are the same but amplified. It's likely that the changes you are experiencing have accelerated in their pace or urgency but not in their kind. Strategy development now may help you to address issues that you needed to address all along, but with more acuity.

9. Strategic planning helps you to reconnect with what's at your core.

COVID-19 will end, and things will re-stabilize. It's likely your mission hasn't changed. Your *"why"* stays true even as your *"how"* is shifting. You are therefore wise to give deliberate thought to how to leverage that new *"how"* without losing sight of your *"why."* That's what strategic planning is all about. And when the shape of the new normal begins to emerge - if you develop some clarity now - you will already have built momentum toward progress markers that are meaningful to you.

10. There's no better time for strategic planning than now.

Things are never not changing. Are you really going to abandon planning until your context becomes more stable and certain? That time may never come. As Roger Martin muses,

> "*If the future is too unpredictable and volatile to make strategic choices, what would lead a manager to believe that it will become significantly less so?*"[4]

You are better to learn to stay looking down the long road even when it's bumpy than waiting for it to smooth out before doing so.

11. Old strategies are now out-of-date.

Continuing with the past plan is now irrelevant. The world has changed too profoundly for you to carry on with business as usual. If you thought this was a year to dust off or tweak your old plan, it isn't. Going back to the way things were is not a viable option, so the likely relevance of your old plan *(if you had one)* in the new world is very low.

12. Strategic intention beats strategic perfection.

Nobody can predict the future with a high degree of accuracy. Your crystal ball has always been broken. Although it seems particularly difficult to predict the future with any accuracy right now, it's important to recognise that we never could. Strategic planning has

---

4 Roger L. Martin, "The Big Lie of Strategic Planning," Harvard Business Review (January-February 2014) https://hbr.org/2014/01/the-big-lie-of-strategic-planning

never been about being clairvoyant. It's about being insightful and intentional, disciplined and responsive. Those skills are future proof.

So, let's continue to plan. Explicitly, deliberately and collaboratively. Planning that is done together, out loud and on purpose is never wasted, in terms of its process or its product.

But we do need to do it differently, in terms of pace and time horizon. We need to increase our cadence and shorten our increments. If the road we're travelling on is winding, we might not be able to look miles ahead. But we certainly should be looking around the next bend.

Five years used to be the traditional strategic planning rhythm. This stemmed from an expectation that we were travelling down an endless highway, and the future was stable and predictable over time. *(That seems like naivete or hubris using today's lenses, doesn't it?)* It also reflected the pragmatism of good stewardship, because fulsome strategic planning takes time to do and even longer to implement, people wanted more breathing space in their planning cycles. Five years allowed for a better return on investment, especially if it took the first half year to develop the plan in the first place. In recent years, that timeframe shortened to three years as the pace of life accelerated and people became less confident in their ability to predict the future. Now, I'm seeing one-year detailed plans – or perhaps as brief as a quarter.

Relevance is of critical concern to organizations not just once in a generation but even once per year.

Those compressed plans are being situated within a longer sightline of perhaps five or ten years – not so much out of a desire to plan for longer as to cast visions that are shorter. Vision statements are being replaced by credos, identity statements or manifestos that read in present tense. Purposeful but pragmatic. I suspect the days of lofty visions with timeframes equal to *"forever"* or *"never"* are numbered.

Concurrently, I see the planning cadence radically speeding up. Contexts are complex and rapidly changing, and they're being disrupted in unforeseeable ways. Relevance is of critical concern to organizations not just once in a generation but even once per year. If strategies are therefore being developed much more frequently, perhaps annually or every 18 months, it doesn't make sense to take six to twelve months to do so.

COVID-19 has placed a lot of unexpected twists and turns on our path. But this doesn't mean we should set strategic planning aside until simpler times return. Just like motorcycles, organizations need momentum.

That's why people are planning in shorter stages while looking down a longer road. They're lifting their gaze to make sure their short-term plans are taking them in a direction they want to go, being pragmatic about the nature of the winding road they're on, and getting to where they want to go faster.

Summary:

Responsive leaders can and must engage in strategic planning in times of uncertainty.

Clarity about your "why" allows you to adapt your "how" when things get crazy. Know your destination but flex on your routes to get there.

Planning needs to happen at a faster pace and shorter increments, inside a longer-term sightline.

Questions:

1. How strategic was your organization prior to the pandemic, and how content would you be to emerge the same way?
2. Which of the 12 reasons listed above are compelling enough to spur you into action?
3. To what extent has COVID-19 affected the relevance of your organization's core mission?
4. If your mission is still important, what collaborative planning events or systems could you put in place to achieve that mission in new ways?
5. What would it take for your organization to accelerate the pace of its planning practices and/or to shorten the length of its planning cycles, even temporarily?

About the Author:

Dr Rebecca Sutherns

Dr. Rebecca Sutherns is a Certified Professional Facilitator who promotes nimble leadership. She is a perceptive and dynamic speaker and author whose insight is grounded in over 25 years of experience as a strategic coach and trusted advisor to hundreds of mission-driven organizations around the world. Her expertise is deepest in facilitating collaborative decision-making. She is a quick learner, creative thinker and skilled communicator, with a particular gift for helping leaders make wiser decisions faster. This content has been adapted from her forthcoming book, Sightline: Strategic plans that gather momentum not dust. Visit rebeccasutherns.com to learn more.

CHAPTER ELEVEN

Trust

Paul Matthews

In 2020, the world was turned upside down for leaders. The first six *(felt like sixty!)* months of the year created global uncertainty on most fronts. The pandemic has knocked many of our norms out of shape. We are operating and communicating in a different style and using different platforms.

As leaders, we are still working without a clear view of what is coming next:

- We need to move forward - but it's unclear how *(not if)* we should.
- And we need to rally and unite and excite employees in a new way of work - but how do we do this through the complexities and uncertainties we're facing?

Throughout the pandemic we have witnessed some outstanding examples of employee behaviour that have saved and changed lives. Humanity shone brightly in the darkness. Many employees have found real purpose during chaos - going above and beyond their position descriptions to rapidly innovate ingenious solutions to address some of the huge issues created by this pandemic.

In time, it will be front-line employees *(not managers or leaders)* that discover and develop vaccines to protect humans from future pandemics - including any potential vaccine to solve the COVID crisis itself.

The pandemic has invigorated employees with purpose that has seen them reach new heights. But why are we seeing so much employee-driven innovation now? Where was this capability hiding prior to the pandemic? And how can leaders harness this innovative employee-driven energy to create clarity and certainty, engagement and excitement around the path ahead?

The answer to all of these questions is hidden in *the Trust Gap*.

Mind the Trust Gap

Creating trust lifts performance. Research has shown that no other aspect of leader behaviour has such a large impact on profits [1]. Our need to trust and be trusted has a very real economic impact. More than that, it deeply affects the fabric of business because if we

1 Frei, F. and Morriss, A., 2020. Everything Starts with Trust. Harvard Business Review, [online] (May-June 2020). Available at: <https://hbr.org/2020/05/begin-with-trust> [Accessed 9 August 2020].

do not trust our leaders, we can't possibly work together to build anything, including a better future[2].

Unfortunately, many leadership teams still see the type of communication that builds trust as an 'optional extra' or as telling employees what to do. This may go some way to explaining why 70% of change projects fail and why just 16% of employees are said to be engaged[3]. A lack of trust contributes to poor industrial relations, low productivity and negatively impacts reputation and performance.

Having trust-building communication as an 'optional extra' means that trust might not always exist, because the key elements that build trust - empathy, authenticity and logic - are not present. Loyalty and belonging are not nurtured. This trust gap between a leader's communication style and the team's needs impacts results, commitment and ultimately reduces leader, employee, and organisational effectiveness.

2 Sucher, S. and Gupta, S., 2019. The Trust Crisis. Harvard Business Review, [online] (July 2019). Available at: <https://hbr.org/cover-story/2019/07/the-trust-crisis> [Accessed 9 August 2020].

3 Perry, M., 2019. Engagement Around the World, Charted. Harvard Business Review, [online] (May 2019). Available at: <https://hbr.org/2019/05/engagement-around-the-world-charted> [Accessed 9 August 2020].

WHAT IS A TRUST GAP?

Trust gaps are sad places with disconnected employees or managers in them. They exist in parts of the business where leaders are not communicating well.

When there are multiple trust gaps in a company, it becomes unstable and unable to support itself. The gaps impact performance and engagement. In time, the gaps become more obvious and show up in the form of operational errors, complaints, accidents or worse.

Humanisation: Closing the Trust Gap

We need to work through the fog of 2020 to help our employees commit and see what is ahead. We need to empower them to feel safe so that they can take action and move forward. They need to trust us for this to happen.

"Employees in high-trust companies are more productive, are more satisfied with their jobs, put in greater discretionary effort, are less likely to search for new jobs, and even are healthier than those working in low-trust companies"[4].

Successful leadership communication that engages the workforce balances direction-setting *(vision)* and involvement *(action)*. The direction-setting brings clarity to individuals and teams. It unites them behind a common purpose.

4 Zac, P., 2019. How our Brains Decide When to Trust. Harvard Business Review, [online] (May 2019). Available at: <https://hbr.org/2019/05/engagement-around-the-world-charted> [Accessed 9 August 2020].

When leader communication is on point, team productivity increases by 22%, performance by 25% and turnover reduces by 65%[5]. Involving employees shows that you value them, their ideas, views, and contribution. Combining these two factors creates an employee conversation that builds trust: putting some of that rocket fuel in the tank, right now, is vital for leaders.

Whether due to the pandemic in 2020, disruptive technologies, economic shifts, or other events, our businesses are experiencing constant change and will continue to do so.

If our employees can become rocket-powered in spite of the chaos of a pandemic, then I wonder what we could achieve daily with high trust and clear direction. So instead of waiting for another crisis to re-humanise us, I say we make trust-building part of our day-to-day communication now, for good.

But how do we do this? How do we overcome the trust gap - humanise organisations - and build close connections and better communication between all members of a team?

Is your communication style LIFTING or LIMITING trust?

Consider the degree of direction setting and the level of involvement your communication creates in your team or workforce. What type of leadership styles do you rise to, and fall back on, as a leader yourself?

---

5 Mann, A. and Darby, R., 2014. Should Managers Focus on Performance or Engagement?. Gallup Business Journal, [online] Available at: <https://news.gallup.com/businessjournal/174197/managers-focus-performance-engagement.aspx> [Accessed 9 August 2020].

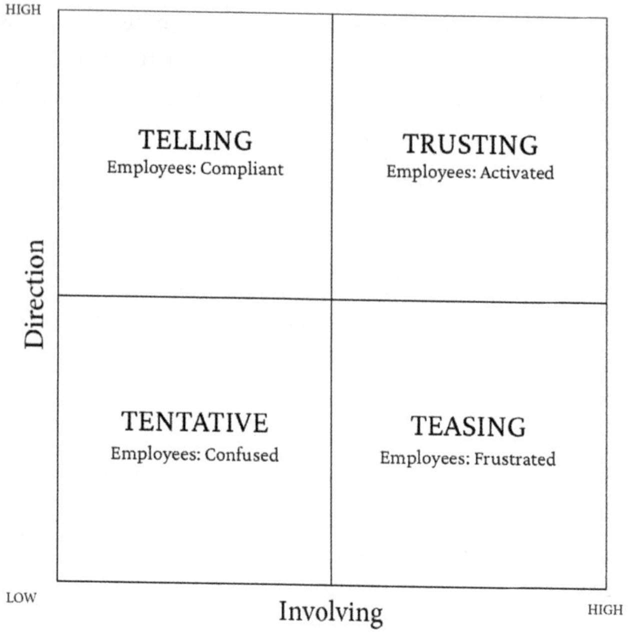

Figure 9: Communication Styles

Telling:

In times of crisis, many leaders switch their communication style to TELLING to assert control. This works in a crisis. However, TELLING or command and control *(coercive leadership)* has been proven as the least effective of leadership styles for everyday business[1]. Forbes contributor Liz Ryan points out that telling, now, is the leadership equivalent to a fax machine[1]. The workforce of the 2020s is educated and empowered. They expect leaders to listen

1 Ryan, L., 2016. Command-And-Control Management Is For Dinosaurs. Forbes, [online] Available at: <https://www.forbes.com/sites/lizryan/2016/02/26/command-and-control-management-is-for-dinosaurs/#50d9f2f324ed> [Accessed 9 August 2020].

and involve. Control and fear, caused by TELLING, dehumanises employees and shuts them down. Right now, employees and organisations need involvement and direction if they are to trust and support leaders.

Teasing:

Spending too much time involving and consulting suggests that a leader cannot decide. They appear to be TEASING as they are seeking insight and ideas but failing to take action. Leaders who seek involvement but fail to give direction often mistake giving employees a voice *(which creates trust)* with giving them a vote, which delays decisions and lacks direction. This creates inaction, misalignment and erodes trust. More direction setting by leaders will engage employees, drive up performance and trust.

Tentative:

When leaders lack both direction and involvement their communication is confusing and TENTATIVE. Instead of moving forward they are flip-flopping on how to lead or engage and end up going nowhere. These leaders are unclear on vision and action, and this confuses their team. Increased direction and involvement in communication will grow more trust and increase support.

Trusting:

While setting clear direction, leaders who involve their team in decisions, listen to their needs, and empower them to make decisions and solve problems have a communication style that is TRUSTING.

This approach activates employees who feel safe, take ownership, and go the extra mile.

Leading Trusted Teams

Building trust is not glamorous or easy. I recently interviewed Bronwyn Evans, CEO of Engineers Australia, about how leaders can become better at listening to gain employee trust, who said:

> "*Sit with the discomfort of not talking for a while and just listen. This can be hard for those not used to doing it, but it is very rewarding. It is uncomfortable at first. You do not have to say yes to everything you hear. Acknowledge what you hear. Stop thinking you need to know all the answers.*"
>
> -Bronwyn Evans, CEO, Engineers Australia

Communication and trust-building are consistently recognised as vital skills for leaders. Business change, transformation or recovery from crises are significantly improved with effective leader communication[2]. For effective leaders, communicating trust has become HOW they lead: part of how they do business. Not an optional extra.

Trusted leaders systematically set direction, listen, ask questions, and empower employees. They have meaningful conversations: they do not tell. They present problems for employees to solve rather than drive compliance with their own ideas. They recognise that employees can add valuable insights and know the business and customers well.

---

2 Matthews, P., 2020. Powerful Communication For Leaders. [online] Sydney. Available at: <https://paulmatthews.com.au/powerful> [Accessed 9 August 2020].

Bronwyn's advice can help leaders embody the style of leadership that engenders trust. It's the type of communication that humanises everyone, creates authentic connection, empowers leaders to be empathetic, and empowers employees. When leaders choose to involve employees and complement this with a clear and empowering direction, it doesn't take long to see positive change.

Thankfully, communication, like leadership, is not genetic. It is learnt. This means that building trust is something every leader can do. The following tools are designed to help you humanise your communication in a busy, remote, and often chaotic new normal. Humanising now will get you ahead and improve resilience for future upheaval or transformation.

Humanising Communication: Building Trust in 3 Practical Steps

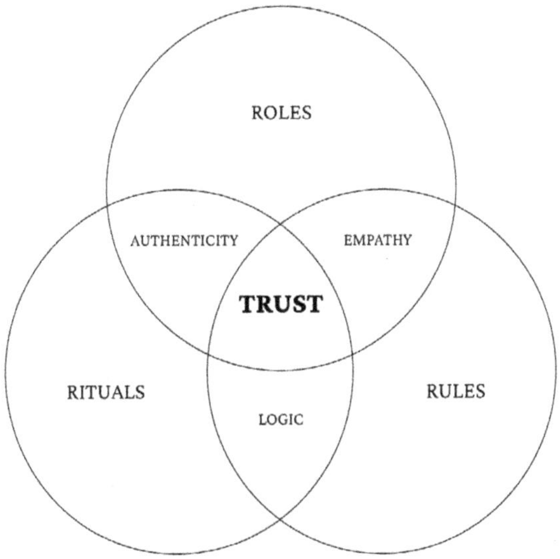

Figure 10: Building Trust

To build trust[3] as a leader, your communication needs to show:

- that you care *(empathy)*
- your rationale *(logic)*
- yourself *(authenticity)*

Empathy

Show that you care, use EMPATHY when you:

- Reinforce your role and the roles of your employees
- Get crystal clear on contribution and action: hold everyone accountable
- Empower employees to take risks, make decisions, implement change.

Empathy in Action at BPAY:

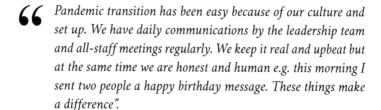

> “*Pandemic transition has been easy because of our culture and set up. We have daily communications by the leadership team and all-staff meetings regularly. We keep it real and upbeat but at the same time we are honest and human e.g. this morning I sent two people a happy birthday message. These things make a difference”.*

- John Banfield CEO, BPAY

Logic

---

3 Frei, F. and Morriss, A., 2020. Everything Starts with Trust. Harvard Business Review, [online] (May-June 2020). Available at: <https://hbr.org/2020/05/begin-with-trust> [Accessed 9 August 2020].

Explain your decisions using LOGIC to:

- Reinforce boundaries, values and performance
- Focus on what matters, let go of low-level stuff
- Ensure everyone understands where they are heading and why.

Logic in Action at Bunnings:

> “*We have really increased connection during the pandemic. Senior Leader phone hook-ups have been happening weekly. We have been doing fortnightly LiveStreams from one of our stores. We have increased connection with our top 200 leaders to really help them explain the reasoning behind our decisions. The rationale is really important.*”

- Michael Schneider, CEO, Bunnings *(April 2020)*

Authenticity

Be AUTHENTIC when you are:

- Uniting the team in shared priorities, activity and conversations
- Creating safe spaces to ask and fail
- Consistently focusing on learning and growth.

Authenticity in Action at BPAY:

> “*I run a CEO roundtable every month with 16 employees. No agenda. Ask anything you like. It is one hour long, and the time*

just flies by. We have a great discussion about what is on people's minds". - John Banfield, CEO BPAY (April 2020)

TRUST BUILDERS: some simple actions every leader can start today

Trust Builders	Asking...	Saying...
Empathy: Show you care	How are you? Do you feel better? How did that meeting go?	I understand how you feel.. I feel the same.... I am happy for you....
Logic: Show rationale	Have I explained that well? Shall I explain it differently? Does that make sense?	We are doing this because... My reasoning was.... The data tells me....
Authenticity: Show yourself	What could I improve on? What should I do more of? What should I do less of?	I am sorry.... I don't know.... I didn't realise....

Solving the Trust Gap Helps Everyone

Employee trust is like rocket fuel for leaders and business. It acts like a catalyst for innovation, change, growth and customer satisfaction. For teams to work together to achieve their goals, particularly in challenging times, leaders must have the trust of their people. If they are trusted, they will get more power to achieve more. Conversely, employees will not follow a leader they do not trust.

The events of 2020 have challenged our ability to connect and involve our team. I believe that if we humanise our communication and leadership now, we will create greater belonging and build more trust. This makes anything possible in future.

Summary:

By listening, involving, and humanising our communication, we can lock in trust-building as part of leading.

Doing this means our relationships deepen, become more resilient and resourceful, because we show we care, show our rationale, and show our true selves.

Building trust is what is going to help us rebuild and restore after the pandemic. Humanising our leadership consistently will put lots of rocket fuel in the tank, ready for future change and challenge.

Questions:

1. Which style leader/communicator are you: TELLING, TENTATIVE, TEASING or TRUSTING?
2. Are you asking and saying in a way that humanises yourself and others?
3. Are you using the right communication channels to build trust?
4. Are you showing you care, your rationale and your true self?
5. How will you ensure these humanising traits stick?

About the Author:

Paul Matthews

Paul Matthews helps leaders activate the workforce by adding rocket fuel to employee conversations, so that leaders can go further faster. He spent 20 years as a corporate communication and leader adviser in large, change resistant, complex businesses.

Working across almost every sector and level has informed Paul's mission to help leaders embed communication in the way they lead, not leave it out as an optional extra.

He works with senior leaders to help them unite and excite their workforce. He helps leaders switch communication style from one way telling, to powerful conversations that energise employees.

Ring 0458 566 179
Click www.paulmatthews.com.au
Write paul@commscoach.org

Act III: Emergence

Support

The hero goes through her own awakening and comes out willing to accept help from others.

CHAPTER TWELVE

Belong

Fiona Robertson

Jeff leads a team of eight, most of whom have their own direct reports, working inside a large, complex organisation. He spends endless hours trying to get his people to work effectively with each other and with other teams. He's getting nowhere fast.

Jeff has lost count of the number of times he's had a member of his team come to him and complain about an issue they're having with one of their colleagues being unsupportive or difficult. If he steps in and tries to broker a truce, it invariably turns into a game of 'you said/they said' and further damages the relationship between them. If he raises the contentious issue in a team meeting, no-one says anything, or they all say everything's fine – but he knows it's not fine.

He has tried several things to get the team to work better together. Once he had them all work on a team purpose statement, and another time they agreed to a set of team values. But in the end the words they'd crafted had no relationship with what was actually happening in the team. Worse, they were often used as 'helpful' reminders from one team member to another about how they were somehow failing to live up to the ideal of the value. This just made the relationships between the team members even more strained.

The tension between Jeff's team members makes everything they do harder. Every decision takes longer than it needs to because the debates are fuelled by interpersonal frustrations instead of genuine concern for getting the best outcome for customers and the organisation. They waste so much time on power struggles. Stress levels are always high because no-one is convinced that the others are well-intentioned, so they endlessly second guess the motives behind their colleagues' actions. It's completely exhausting, feels horrible and stops them from performing anywhere near as well as they could.

Jeff would give anything for his people to help each other more and to work more effectively with other teams. He wants them to have each other's backs and sort through problems together; maybe even have some fun. And he would dearly love to not have to play 'dad' in what feels like an endless game of sibling rivalry.

Why can't Jeff get any traction? Because he's solving the wrong problem. He's trying to shift his team's behaviour just by using 'surface level' devices such as values. What he doesn't understand – what most people don't understand, actually – is that values and culture are not the same thing. Values work at an individual level. Culture is what happens under the surface of interactions in the spaces between people. It lurks in the interpretation of behaviour, not in the behaviour itself. It can be seen, but only if you know where to look. Once you start to see it, you will never be able to un-see it. You will have the code to unlock the secret of culture.

Culture is one of the most widely discussed and yet widely misunderstood concepts in business today. Greater focus from regulators and boards in the last few years has created a whole lot of extra activity around culture, but most of this activity will have very little impact other than to make us look like we're doing something.

Many confuse culture with employee engagement. Measuring culture is measuring the underlying system; measuring engagement is measuring our employees' experience of that system. They are not the same thing.

Culture is about the rules of belonging. It's in the underlying patterns of 'what it takes to earn belonging' in organisations. The rules of belonging determine the behaviours that increase a person's status and acceptance in a particular group at a specific time.

We can all identify the rules of belonging within a remarkably short time of joining a new group. However, once we've been in a group for a while, they become part of our environment and we no longer notice them - when you're immersed in a culture, it's almost impossible to see.

Humans are hard-wired to seek to belong - relationship needs are one of the most important needs that humans must fulfill. Throughout time, our brains have kept us alive by helping us quickly figure out how to adapt our behaviour to belong in the groups we join. We're especially motivated to use our evolutionary super-powers of observation when we join a new work tribe because a whole lot of our status, not to mention our livelihood, is at risk if we don't quickly adapt to belong.

We behave our way to earning belonging. Understanding this process is the key to understanding how to successfully change culture. It typically starts with examining a new culture, and ends in enforcing it:

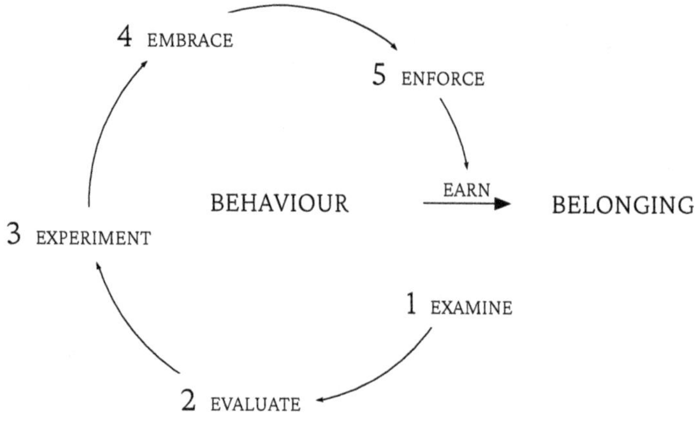

Figure 11: Behaving our way to Belonging

Examine

First, we examine. We observe what others do and say, what they wear, what time they arrive at work and what time they leave, how they speak in meetings, the kind of work outputs they produce, what they say in front of senior people, how they lead their teams and who they eat lunch with.

Evaluate

After we've watched others for a while, we evaluate by determining which of their behaviours gains them more versus less status and belonging. We see how those with power react to the behaviours we've been examining. When someone is always one of the first to arrive at work each morning, is this effort admired or are they seen as trying to make an impression?

When someone produces a presentation pack full of graphs and charts, does the team praise their ability to express complex data in meaningful ways, or do they roll their eyes and make comments about 'death by PowerPoint'? Is the person who consistently wears a suit seen as more professional?

The responses to these situations will vary in each place of employment and will vary over time. There will also be different responses in different organisations at the same point in time, though the differences will be more subtle. These nuances matter enormously. Those skilled at picking them up are more likely to earn belonging.

Experiment

We examine and evaluate constantly throughout our working days. When we've seen enough of a particular behaviour to believe that it will be met with approval and will enhance our status and belonging, we try it out ourselves. This phase is all about experimentation. We try it and see what happens. In a culture where an early start appears to receive respect, we start arriving earlier and earlier. In a culture where PowerPoint is king, we brush up on our graph creation skills.

In a culture where people in tailored suits gain more recognition, we start to pay more attention to how we show up.

Embrace

If a behaviour we adopt creates the approval and belonging we hoped for, we will embrace and continue that particular behaviour. We slowly adopt a set of behaviours that makes us blend in with the norms of the group we have joined, and feel an increasing sense of belonging. As time goes by, we further refine our behaviours, tweaking them to ensure they still apply as we progress. All the while deepening our sense of being a fully-fledged, welcome and embraced member of the tribe, and by default, ensuring that we have more and more to lose if the rules of belonging were to change.

This is vital. If the rules of belonging begin to change, then the things that have made us belong might start to be frowned upon. When this happens, we risk losing the belonging we have worked so hard to earn. Our brains interpret this as a significant threat to our survival.

One of my favourite researchers is Matthew Lieberman, Professor of Psychology, Psychiatry and Biobehavioral Sciences at UCLA. He is also the Director of UCLA's Social Cognitive Neuroscience Lab. In his book 'Social', he says *"When human beings experience threats or damage to their social bonds, the brain responds in much the same way it responds to physical pain."*

We're so hard-wired for belonging that, consciously or unconsciously, we will expend significant effort to ensure we protect the belonging that we have. Sadly, what this means in some organisations is that when someone new arrives and suggests that there might be a better or different way to do something, we may appear as though we're listening and interested, but find small ways to make it clear we're not too sure about their idea.

Enforce

New people and new ways of doing things threaten our belonging. They threaten our status and our safety. Knowingly or unknowingly, we work to ensure that things stay more or less the way they were – or at least close enough to ensure our way of doing things remains the best way to guarantee our continued status, belonging and acceptance. We enforce the status quo culture that we worked so hard to conform to as a means of self-protection.

Dr David Rock, the co-founder of the NeuroLeadership Institute, in his book Your Brain at Work wrote that *"a sense of decreasing status can feel like your life is in danger."*

It isn't as simple as 'people don't like change'. Resistance to change is a perfectly rational response to a threat that feels very real. Humans are spectacularly good at change in the service of our own belonging. Just think about how quickly we change our behaviour when we get a new boss.

The change we have seen on a global scale in a matter of weeks through the early stages COVID-19 has been truly breathtaking.

When Everything Changes, Change Everything

Due to the stages above, culture can be incredibly resilient - whether positive or negative. As leaders, we need to understand that the dynamics of culture and the rules of belonging are a powerful force. If your culture aligns with your ambitions as an organisation, it will turbo-charge your performance, but if there is a misalignment between culture and strategy, culture will always overwhelm the strategy. If you feel that your organisational culture isn't consistent with your purpose, then there has never been a better time to influence change. This is an opportunity to break what have become traditions and ways of working that are not serving us or our organisations.

For years I've heard directors and executives lament the fact that they don't have a 'burning platform', a catalyst that will motivate and energise their people and focus them on making the changes they need to make. A reason to stop operating on autopilot, take a moment to notice what they're doing and consciously decide whether or not it is working. After all, you have to notice before you can choose.

We didn't ask for COVID-19, but there's no denying that while we are exposed to the horror of a pandemic, it offers us a significant opportunity for reflection.

Most organisations are in the process of rethinking their strategy in some form or other. Whether it's who they target, what they offer or how they go to market, they're checking to make sure their unique combination of 'who, what, how' still makes sense as we establish a COVID-safe world. More than ever, they're becoming curious about their 'why'.

What is the meaning behind our work? What contribution do we make to the world beyond making money? All of that reflection is as essential for organisational performance as it is for our collective sanity.

What some organisations have forgotten is that a new strategy, without the culture to execute it successfully, is just a piece of paper. Strategy and culture are two parts of one thing. They are always changing and must continuously reinforce each other in an endless loop.

Rebuilding organisational culture post-COVID-19

Your culture is changing. Right now. Whether you're actively managing it or not, it will happen.

It's easy to underestimate how tribal humans are. As the ultimate social species, we're hard-wired to keep ourselves safe through belonging and connection, so the recent cognitive dissonance of staying apart to stay safe is intensely unsettling. Our tribes are dispersing and reforming far faster than usual and this adds to our feeling that we're under threat.

Our sense of belonging has been fundamentally disrupted, and it's less clear right now what the rules of belonging are. Like the Kurt Lewin model, the rules will 'unfreeze - change - refreeze'. The new rules of belonging may support and accelerate our new strategies or may hinder and delay them. The only way to know is to be deliberate about it, and to identify the behaviours we need more of and less of, and put in place clear actions to ensure they shift in the right direction. This happens most effectively through explicit, specific conversations with our people about what worked in the old world that will and won't work in the new. Then we need to put in place new rituals and build new tribes who embrace and reinforce what the new good looks like around here; our new rules of belonging.

If you want to change the culture, you need to change the rules of belonging.

Summary:

If you understand what the rules of belonging are in your team today, you can understand how your team culture works, and how to change it. You do this by:

Identifying the current rules of belonging

Figuring out which of those rules are encouraging helpful behaviours and which are not

Designing an intervention to shift the rules of belonging so they encourage the behaviours that are helpful for your team and discourage the ones that are unhelpful

Questions:

1. When you're debating new strategies, how actively are you considering whether or not you have the culture to execute them?
2. When you're working on improving your culture, how much of your focus is on creating a culture that will turbo-charge your strategy rather than just make your people feel good?
3. What behaviours do you need to see more of and less of to ensure your new strategy can be implemented successfully?
4. What was great about your culture before the pandemic that you want to take forward beyond it?
5. What improved about your culture during the pandemic that you want to keep, nurture and grow?

About the Author:

Fiona Robertson

Fiona Robertson is the former Head of Culture for the National Australia Bank and a sought-after culture change and leadership speaker, facilitator, coach and author who helps leaders create cultures people really want to belong to.

Her first book, 'Rules of Belonging - change your organisational culture, delight your people and turbo-charge your results', is published by Major Street Publishing. More articles are available on www.fionarobertson.com

CHAPTER THIRTEEN

Connect

Celeste Halliday

We're all being called on to do something significant right now. Something that takes us out of the current chaos and ambiguity of the COVID-19 pandemic, and into a brighter future. We're all looking for a key. Luckily, a key is right in front of us – hiding in plain sight.

Every single significant achievement throughout human history has been accomplished through people sharing a vision and working together to bring it to life. This holds true for us, as leaders, now. Connecting with a vision. Connecting to each other.

Connection is the key that's hiding in plain sight – right in front of, and inside, each of us. We already have the key but somewhere along the way we lost sight of how deeply important it is, and how to use it.

A friend recently told me about a radio interview with a remarkable older person named Edna. Edna is 100 years old. She's already lived through two world wars and now two pandemics. She knows a thing or two about shifting out of surviving and into thriving, which is what we want to do with our teams. Edna emphasised the power of human connection as our way through;

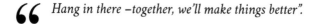

> “ *Hang in there –together, we'll make things better".*

The COVID-19 pandemic is stripping away many things, yet it's also shining fresh light on this most human of skills. We're seeing beautiful examples every day of neighbours helping neighbours, and we're being invited into the lounge rooms of our teams and colleagues, and meeting their children and pets in a way we never would have before. We're all in this together. That's our power. The leaders who embrace it, and master it, are the ones we will follow to a better tomorrow.

We need to remember that whilst the pandemic is new to us, there are many examples of leaders who've led through similar times before that we can look to and learn from.

Andrew, a high profile Australian CEO who I work with, is one of those. Andrew is super smart, hard-working and a great leader.

Some years ago, he and his team had just put an ambitious strategy in place, when their market began to decline rapidly. The writing was on the wall, just like it is now, that troubled times were ahead.

Andrew was doing all the things a 'good' leader should do to guide his team through the change – new plans and priorities, all executed at pace, in response to the market. Yet it felt overwhelming. Every day his team were pulled into back-to-back meetings, gasping for space between waves of tasks. Their work hours blew out and when they were with their families they were distracted with the chaos of work. It felt disjointed from their strategy, and they felt isolated and disconnected from each other as they each tried to turn their own areas around.

Fast forward a year and they'd crossed over to an entirely different space. They'd delivered the seemingly unachievable, building a bridge out and delivering astounding business results, where others failed. They were closer than ever, their stakeholders gave them brilliant feedback and they reported great work-life balance and sky-high engagement.

The 'bridge' Andrew had built out of the chaos into calm, was connection.

Connection Powers Performance

Connection is the bedrock upon which extraordinary cultures are built. It's the foundation of all great leadership and, in fact, any relationship. It's the glue that holds our teams, families and communities together. It's the key to creating more human leaders and high-performance results.

Connected leaders build connected teams and create connected cultures

At the individual level, connection is the number one predictor of whether someone will thrive both professionally and personally. Several decades of research on social connection have confirmed it's the greatest predictor of long-term happiness and success.[1]

At the group level, in a study of over 80,000 interactions among college students published in the journal *Nature*, the highest achievers were those who formed the most social connections and shared information in more ways. Conversely, research by Ozcelik and Barsade showed how workplace disconnection is directly related to lower job performance.[2]

It makes sense - the more connected we are, the more we achieve, together.

Disconnection

As the pandemic unfolded we all saw the consequences of disconnection in real-time.

Toilet paper and pasta sauce disappeared from supermarket shelves overnight. Fear and blaming – the very human reactions we can all

1 Achor, S, 2011 'The Happy Secret to Better Work', TEDxBloomington, https://www.ted.com/talks/shawn_achor_the_happy_secret_to_better_work?language=en

2 Ozcelik, H, Barsade, S, 2018, 'No Employee an Island: Workplace Loneliness and Job Performance', retrieved 14th July 2020, https://journals.aom.org/doi/10.5465/amj.2015.1066

have to ambiguity, chaos and change were rife. We saw the elderly and vulnerable in tears, unable to buy basic weekly staples. It was heart-breaking, and we all played a role. Let's be honest, we've all sat in judgement of others during this period.

Disconnection starts in fear; when we judge, when we blame or scorn, when we see ourselves as different to or better than others. We forget in our own stress and anxiety that it's our role, as

leaders, to stay calm and show compassion. To be curious about other peoples reactions and what might be driving them. To build bridges to, and between others.

We forget that just like the oxygen mask on a plane, we need to first connect with ourselves as a priority, every day, before we can effectively connect outside.

In our workplaces, we're seeing people struggling with leading and working remotely, feeling uncertain, anxious and alone, not necessarily having the skills to support people from a distance. We're seeing people's energy flatten, despite them still often being productive, and we know that they're starting to disconnect – from the organisation, from our team, from us.

It's hard work to lead through this when we're overwhelmed and over-worked ourselves. It takes a great deal of reflection and thoughtful self-management. In order to solve the meaningful problems we're currently facing, however, connection is our bridge out. Focussing on building connection smooths difficult conversations, it sparks innovation, and builds engagement, discretionary effort and resilience.

So, how do we build this connection bridge, practically?

The 'Connected Leaders System' is built on years of coaching and training leaders and teams like Andrew's. It shows you how to build your bridge into a brighter tomorrow, brick-by-brick. It starts with understanding that we need to connect ourselves and our teams not just with other 'humans', but also with clarity *(your 'Why')*, culture *(your 'How')*, contribution *(your 'What')*, and community *(your 'Who')*. We also need to remember that at each of these levels, we must learn how to connect remotely, now, as well as in person.

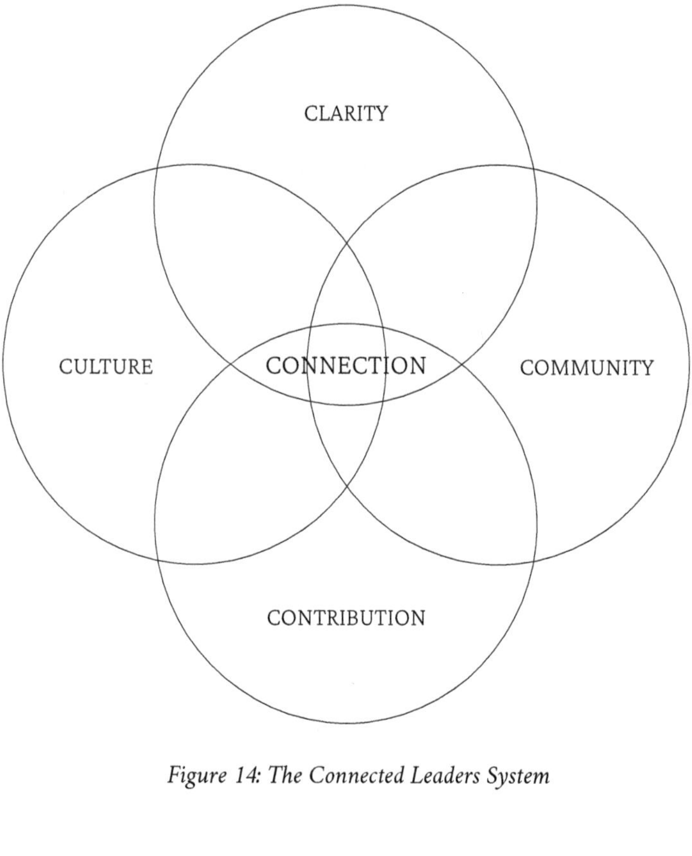

Figure 14: The Connected Leaders System

Connected Leaders System: Part 1: Connecting with Clarity – Your Why

> *"Clarity & simplicity are the antidotes to complexity & uncertainty." - General Andrew Casey* [3]

Stuart is a senior firefighter. He told me that on reaching the chaos of an active fire, before the team 'do' anything, they stop. They assess the situation and get complete clarity on their plan and their roles. Years of life-threatening work has taught them that the only way to save lives and beat the fire is to first get clear about what they're dealing with and aligned on who is doing what.

In times of change, we also need to get laser-focussed and aligned, completely clear on how new priorities integrate, and update our strategy, as required. It means continually reviewing what's important and cutting out what's not, focussing on only the most important things to get us where we need to go now.

There are three steps to connect with Clarity:

1. Crystallise:

---

3 Hogge, T, 2014, 'What I Learned About Leadership from A 4-Star General', retrieved 6th July 2020, https://www.businessinsider.com/leadership-lessons-from-a-4-star-general-2014-11?IR=T

Clarity isn't a process you can 'set and forget' once a year. It's a discipline we create on a quarterly, weekly and daily basis.

Take the time to review where you and your team are actually spending your time. Understand your 'one most important thing' – and do it, first thing, every day.

2. Course correct and cut:

Keep track to see when you and your team are getting caught up with 'noisy', urgent priority changes and keep ruthlessly re-prioritising. Now is a great time to re-invent meetings, streamline processes and cut out what doesn't count. Especially when working remotely, make meetings short, sharp and human.

3. Communicate:

Many of us assume our teams know what they're doing and why, but in periods of change it pays to invest extra time ensuring our thinking, direction and communication are 100% clear. Connecting your team and the work they're doing to the purpose of the organisation – the why – is a critical driver of engagement and high-performance. We need to make this connection with every person in our team, every day.

Connected Leaders System: Part 2: Connecting with Culture – Your How

> *"When we feel safe inside the organization, we will naturally combine our talents and our strengths and work tirelessly to face the dangers outside and seize the opportunities." - Simon Sinek* [4]

During difficult periods, we need to dial-up our focus on culture and values and be aware that building culture remotely takes extra work.

It's easy to lose sight of a declining culture when we're remote, and we need to be alert to the signals that we're losing connection.

One way to do this is to conduct an informal 'culture temperature check' using our 'Positivity, Trust & Psychological Safety' model below. These are the fundamentals of a 'Connected Culture'. You can do this as a self-reflection or even better, involve your team and discuss each area with them, individually or as a team.

1. Prioritising Productivity:

Research indicates that all performance and business outcomes improve when we're positive; our brains are 30% more intelligent, resilient and creative when we're positive, than when we're negative, neutral or stressed. [5]

4 Sinek, S, 2014, 'Why Good Leaders Make You Feel Safe', https://www.youtube.com/watch?time_continue=2&v=lmyZMtPVodo&feature=emb_title

5 Achor, S, 2011 'The Happy Secret to Better Work', TEDxBloomington, https://www.ted.com/talks/shawn_achor_the_happy_secret_to_better_work?language=en

As Shawn Achor and Michelle Gielan, positive psychology experts and authors note, this is even more important during times of challenge and change, when; *"...leaders should be actively encouraging positivity because it will help teams weather the storm"*.[6]

We can role model a hopeful, optimistic outlook, whilst also acknowledging that times are tough. We want our teams firmly in the space of looking for opportunities and improvements, not feeling helpless and hopeless.

Review the language in all communication and add a celebration/wins/recognition section on every team and project agenda – 'where focus goes, energy flows.'

2. Targeting Trust & Strengthening Safety:

Think about your recent meetings, was everyone engaged and participating, openly discussing ideas, issues and failures, giving each other feedback and asking for help? If not, you need to understand why and what needs to change.

When people are scared, they can react in less than positive ways, shutting down the very ideas and innovations we need. Focus on actively creating a climate of safety and openness in your team. Encourage candour and input - and very importantly, respond positively when you get it!.

6 Achor, S, Gielan, M, 2020 'What Leading with Optimism Really Looks Like' https://hbr.org/2020/06/what-leading-with-optimism-really-looks-like

To do this, we must role model authenticity and vulnerability ourselves – admit mistakes, ask for and listen to feedback and re-build trust where we've damaged it. We need to intervene where we see failures blamed on individuals, people shamed for speaking up or sharing ideas and cliquey noninclusive behaviour. This is even harder to spot when we're working remotely, so we need to take the time to ask each person in the team how safe they feel to share ideas and what we need to do to improve.

Connected Leaders System: Part 3: Connecting with Contribution – Your What

> “*Genius is in the idea. Impact, however, comes from action.*”
> *Simon Sinek*[7]

During periods of change, priorities can shift quickly. It's easy to lose sight of why we're doing what we do. Our days can become a series of tasks to tick off, as we lose connection with the meaning and purpose of our work and the impact our contribution makes.

Reinforce why each person's work matters to the vision. The more our team can see the direct impact of their contribution, the more confident they'll feel - and the more competent they'll then become. In his book 'Drive', Daniel Pink summarises this as improving 'autonomy, mastery and purpose'.[8]

---

7 Sinek, S, 2014, 3rd December, <https://www.facebook.com/simon-sinek/posts/genius-is-in-the-idea-impact-however-comes-from-action/10152902575386499/>, retrieved 17th July 2020

8 Pink, D, 2011, 'Drive', 1st Edition, Penguin Putnam Inc, United States

Use the three steps below, inspired by this research, to connect your people to the contribution they're making in your next one-on-one meeting.

1. Know:

Focus on coaching each person in what they need to know to do their job well. Understand where they're trying to develop – both role specific and leadership skills - to help them improve.

2. Show:

Link each person's current work to the meaning and purpose of why the work matters to the customer, and the impact they are personally having. Make their progress and development visible to them and to the broader business.

3. Grow:

Encourage each person's ownership of their work, role and development. Believe and trust they can do it. Tell them and show them that you do.

Connected Leaders System: Part 4: Connecting with Community – Your Who

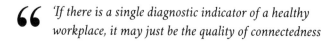

> “ *'If there is a single diagnostic indicator of a healthy workplace, it may just be the quality of connectedness*

> *and ease of idea flow that characterizes them.' - Margaret Heffernan*[9]

When was the last time you really thought about who you're connected with and who your team are connecting with?

To innovate our way out of chaos and change, we need as many, diverse experiences and ideas as possible. Great ideas can come from anywhere, and we need to focus on building connections within, and importantly, outside of the team and even the organisation to open up possibilities for new ideas, development and growth.

Sometimes people are unsure of how to start. Encourage them to use the below 'Give, Get, Grow' questions to expand their connections. Encourage them to answer them for their immediate team, the broader business and even wider, outside of the business to the broader community.

1. Give:

- What skills have I got to share?
- Where could I provide a different perspective to help diversify someone's thinking?
- What help can I give? To Who?

2. Get:

- What help do I need? Who might have this?

---

9 Heffernan, M, 2015, 'Beyond Measure: The Big Impact of Small Changes', 1st Edition, Simon & Schuster, United Kingdom

- What interests do I have, or want to develop, that others might have?

3. Grow:

- What skills do I need to develop? Who might help with this?
- How can I diversify my thinking?

Build Your Bridge

As a leader, during challenging times, it's tempting to bunker down and wait for the storm to pass. To do your best to simply survive - and leave thriving for another day. However, the best leaders I've worked with have forged their skills during difficult times, like these, and you can too.

You already have the one skill you need most, right now. Connection.

Connection will power your performance.

Just like it's powered the performance of leaders at some of the best organisations in the world.

Like them, you can use the Connected Leaders System, outlined in this chapter, as a practical brick-by-brick guide to build your own bridge, just like Andrew did, into a better tomorrow.

Connect with yourself first – get clear, centred and calm. Manage your emotions so your attention is focussed 'out' on your team, clients and stakeholders, rather than on the internal noise of our busy, and reactive, brains.

Make sure you're connected with Clarity - your own purpose, and the organisation's. Hone your vision until it's strong and inspiring. Communicate it so that it unites and engages different people and groups across the organisation and gives them clear guardrails to prioritise work and feel inspired.

Check in on how connected your team Culture is. Understand where people might be disconnecting, especially when working remotely, and connect them back with the vision, strategy and importantly, the Contribution they're making to the team and the customer.

Finally, look at who you could extend your Community to include. Connect with vulnerability and curiosity to the people you lead, your peer groups, stakeholders and clients. Keep those relationships strong and new ideas will begin to flow.

Every great accomplishment has been achieved by people sharing a vision and working together to achieve it.

Connected leaders, building connected teams and creating connected cultures.

Summary:

We need to connect with ourselves, first, before we can connect anywhere else

Start with Clarity (The WHY) and then review the way you're connecting with Culture (The HOW), Contribution (The WHAT) and Community (The WHO)

The Connected Leaders System helps us power performance and harness the collective to think and innovate our way out, together

Questions:

1. How connected am I to the vision of the leader I want to be?
2. How clear am I on where we're going?
3. What am I doing to connect each member of the team, and the work they're doing, to our vision?
4. What would need to change to make it safer to have ideas and try new things in our team?
5. How am I enabling skill and leadership development to help my team stretch themselves and develop further?

About the Author:

Celeste Halliday

Celeste has been working with leaders and their teams for over 25 years, to achieve remarkable results by creating Connected Leaders, Connected Teams & Connected Cultures.

Celeste achieves breakthrough outcomes with the world's most progressive organisations by blending her background in psychotherapy, her fascination with emerging insights from the world of neuroscience and her practical Board & Executive experience in Australia & overseas.

This blend has seen her become a global expert in her field, working as a keynote speaker, facilitator, trainer and mentor.

The Moment of Truth

The hero has found her strength and resolve. Nothing can stop her now.

CHAPTER FOURTEEN

Mindsafety

Dr Amy Silver

How we succeed in the game of life depends on our ability to manage our mindset. We can train our minds to control what we do and how we do it. The alternative is to be controlled by what is happening around us. Without the ability to manage our mindset, we give up our internal power and simply react to our environment.

We live in a volatile, uncertain, complex, and ambiguous world, often shortened to *"VUCA"*. Our simple minds need to function within that. We are emotionally triggered in big ways and small ways every moment of the day. There is a need for us to manage our minds so we are not just reactive, but rather we choose our response. A safe mindset is one that, regardless of what we are experiencing, we can self-manage.

If we allow fear, anger, irritation, sadness, shame - or indeed any of our difficult emotions - to be in control, we are vulnerable to the choices they want us to make. Usually, these emotions have automatic behaviours attached to them, and these can be micro *(small, almost imperceptive behaviours)*, or macro ones. When we are irritated by someone, we may take away our eye contact, hold our breath, shuffle papers and start to gather our stuff to leave the conversation. Potentially we may even mutter to show our irritation, or try to catch other people's eye contact to gain support. When we feel threatened by someone, or by something someone says, we may feel our adrenaline go up. We develop tunnel vision and we may quip back at someone to remind them that we are not a walkover, or to remind them of their place. We may block listening to what they are saying, or put our hand up to deny them more air time.

When we are in fear, we often go to one of two extremes, from being totally consumed by it to trying to deny its very existence. On the one hand, fear can feel like it takes over our brain, consuming our thoughts and telling us what to do - avoid, retreat, keep quiet, blend into the background, and so on. An alternative response to fear is the placing of fear behind a wall and denying its very existence - not only to others, but sometimes to ourselves too! This wall is part of what makes it difficult for people to connect in times of fear, because the wall makes it hard to see the humanity in the other person. Brene Brown's work has shown us the value of increasing vulnerability to enable communication. But how do we increase our vulnerability if we are in fear?

Our fears are necessary, but they are dangerous if we cannot control our response to them. Individually and collectively, performance requires us developing solutions to calm our fears so we can function well at work.

Individual Mindsafety

The core part of our brain that creates our emotional reactions is not that dissimilar to that of a lizard, that's why it has the nickname of 'the reptilian brain'. It is primitively reactive, and is designed to keep us safe. The outer cortex of our brain *(the bit you are familiar with seeing, white and nobbly)* has taken millions of years to develop. It is this part of our brain that is immensely clever. It is so phenomenally complex and powerful that we are yet to find the end of its competencies. Unfortunately for us, the outer cortex is not always in control and our performance both as individuals and as a collective is severely hampered as a result.

We have all experienced loss both in real terms when we have something tangible taken from us, as well as the loss we feel when expectations for the future are dashed. Any unforeseen event will exacerbate our emotions and reduce our capacity to manage them effectively. We are much more likely to allow our reptilian brain to control us to the detriment of our performance.

Being able to calm this part of our brain *(and that of others)* allows the clever part of our brain to push our performance to a high level. When we can create safety mindsets, we have a high level of flexibility as to what we do and that means we can maximise our outcomes. Rather than choosing a behavioural response based on our evolutionary restrictions or our personal habits, we want to be making behavioural responses in line with our goals.

In a work context, two particular focuses need to be considered in terms of expertly calming the primitive brain. Firstly, we must understand how to manage our own mindset, regardless of context.

Secondly, we must understand how to manage ourselves as a group of people working together, as a collective.

Group Mindsafety

Humans are social animals driven by a need to belong and be valued. Psychological safety is the term used to describe the safety that we feel when we are together *(Kahn, 1990[1])*. When in social groups, most people screen others to evaluate if they will be rejected, ridiculed, mistreated, ignored or be insignificant. This drive to be social is often even more pronounced with people in powerful positions. The result is we may keep things to ourselves, or align ourselves with those we feel are accepted by the group *(either because of hierarchy or another characteristic)*. This overwhelming drive to fit in and be social is the reason groups tend to lose cognitive diversity *(different ways of thinking)* as we head towards the safe, average.

When we are in a state of fear, we often conform to the most dominant person, or we head towards less risky decisions or ideas. We double-guess ourselves and hesitate on giving our true ideas or thoughts. We also see a lack of commitment and accountability, difficulties making decisions and little innovation. Perhaps most damaging of all is the lack of shared responsibility for the collective outcome. We protect ourselves at the expense of the outcome.

Even though we have the potential to achieve more when we are together, unfortunately we also have the potential to get distracted by interpersonal friction and inefficient communication. Additionally, decision making can be severely challenged by groupthink *(when we tend towards the same thoughts as each other)*. By mastering our collective mindsets, we have the capability for remarkable outcomes.

---

1 Kahn, W., 1990. Psychological Conditions of Personal Engagement and Disengagement at Work. Academy of Management Journal, 33(4), pp.692-724.

Much attention towards the phenomenon of psychological safety was prompted by Project Aristotle, a project completed by Google to research high performing teams [2]. Rozovsky, the key researcher in this project, concluded that psychological safety was the number one dimension that determined a team's performance. When there is low psychological safety, we don't point out risks or mistakes *(mine or yours)*, we struggle to welcome feedback and honesty, we struggle with accountability and constructive differences, we don't like to do things differently, to come up with new ideas, or to share new ideas.

A lack of psychological safety hampers our communication. At its worst, it becomes combative; we literally cannot communicate with each other without unhealthy conflict. One solution for this, thought not a particularly effective one, is the avoidance of communication. We decide we won't be able to get through it so we just avoid it! This avoids the symptoms, without addressing the cause. Both avoidant and combative communication are unproductive and lead to poor performance.

Many collectives sanitise their conversations out of a desire to be polite and not rock the boat. People will circle conflict, make sure they prioritise 'nice' over difficult conversations and favour 'same' over different. Imagine how many missed opportunities there are for excelling in performance when an organisation is stuck in 'polite mode'? The result is lack of robust conversations, silence or stifled conversations and sweeping things under the carpet. Grossman [3] examined 400 companies with 100,000 employees each and cited

2 Duhigg, C., 2016. What Google Learned From Its Quest to Build the Perfect Team. New York Times Magazine, [online] Available at: <https://www.nytimes.com/2016/02/28/magazine/what-google-learned-from-its-quest-to-build-the-perfect-team.html>.

3 Grossman, D., 2011. The Cost Of Poor Communications. PRovoke Media, [online] Available at: <https://www.provokemedia.com/latest/article/the-cost-of-poor-communications>.

an average loss per company of $62.4 million per year because of inadequate communication to and between employees.

There is an often-held belief that the more intelligent the staff group, the higher the performance. This is not necessarily true; high performing teams can create psychological safety so they can tolerate courageous conversations. The following table shows the relationship between psychological safety and collective intelligence are strongly related *(see table)*. Collective intelligence beats average intelligence.

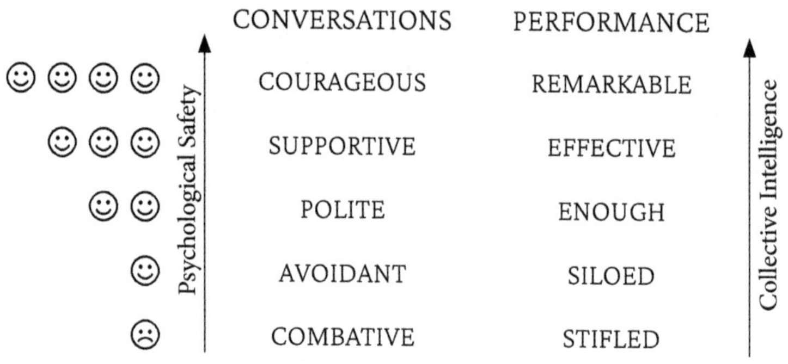
CONVERSATIONS
PERFORMANCE
Psychological Safety
Collective Intelligence
COURAGEOUS
REMARKABLE
SUPPORTIVE
EFFECTIVE
POLITE
ENOUGH
AVOIDANT
SILOED
COMBATIVE
STIFLED

Figure 15: Obsolete to Adaptive

Edmondson, 2012[4] demonstrated the life and death importance of psychological safety in hospital cardiac teams. The research compared teams with high psychological safety *(which tended to lower mortality rates)* with those with low psychological safety *(which tended to high mortality rates)*. Not only can high psychological safety literally save lives, individuals in organisations which have high

4 Edmondson, A., 2012. Teaming. San Francisco, Calif.: Jossey-Bass.

internal trust experience 74% less stress, 106% more energy, 50% more productivity and 73% more engagement *(Zak, 2017)*[5].

We must keep our focus on the fear within an organisation focusing on the individual's mindsafety *(internally driven)* and our collective mindsafety *(externally driven)*. In my programs The Safe Space, each individual is shown how to create their own mindsafety, and each team works through the triggers and behaviours for collective mindsafety. By creating mindsafety for all we can create high performing teaming behaviours. The three crucial elements of this are:

Consciousness:

Our capability to control our responses to our world *(no matter how VUCA it is)*, depends on recognising both the habit we are enacting and recognising the moment of choice to do something else. We want to create a response *(choice-based)*, not a reaction *(no conscious thought)* to challenging events. This life long practice of increasing our consciousness is how we ensure we engage the cleverest part of our brains.

One of the core messages of all the work I do with people is to help them notice the choice point in their behaviour. Most often, our behaviour is an automatic reaction to a trigger or a scenario. We are creatures of habit, and we need predictability as it provides a level of safety. Any behaviour *(good or bad)* that is sanctioned by the collective will be perceived as a safer option for us to avoid rejection. This is how culture is made.

5 Zak, P., 2017. The Neuroscience of Trust. Harvard Business Review, [online] (January-February 2017). Available at: <https://hbr.org/2017/01/the-neuroscience-of-trust>.

Compassion:

When we are compassionate towards each other, we value each other even if we disagree. We take action towards helping each other feel safe. It means we can have courageous conversations without them turning personal. We can build on each other's contribution rather than bring each other down. It is essential for collective intelligence and good social being.

When there is a challenge, taking the time to understand both our own reactions and the reactions of others is essential to managing the primitive brain's response. Within that, we will have to learn how to be more self-compassionate. There must be a tolerance of our own emotions and the ability to not feel ashamed or guilty for having difficult emotions. This is when we can take the increased vulnerability to show our true self. If we are intimidated or scared to speak up, and have a desire to change that, we must come from a place of self-compassion if we are to create safety for ourselves. The alternative *(self-criticism)* only sees us retreat further into fear and shame.

Seeing ourselves and each other as flawed creatures who are trying their best to make sense of their world helps to drive the empathy that we all need to enable us to travel safely through complex scenarios.

Courage:

Courage is action in the face of fear. We act courageously when we choose our behaviour based on what we want, rather than what fear tells us to do.

In terms of performance mindsets, courage looks like:

- Risking failure
- Speaking up rather than staying 'hidden'
- Suggesting something outside the norm
- Showing risks others haven't seen *(or don't want to see)*
- Asking each other to be accountable
- Giving feedback to others
- Receiving or inviting feedback
- Bringing elephants in the room to the table
- Pointing out bad practices in the group *(e.g. lateness for meetings, the dominance of one person, lack of decision making, interpersonal friction etc)*
- Transparency
- Showing vulnerability
- Going first with trust
- Communicating with compassion and candour

Rigid habits, old stories, operating with fixed beliefs will slow down our adaptation. Courage is required if we are to change the status quo. Experimentation and commitment to trying new behaviours, despite the draw to stick to the familiar are how we will develop as individuals and as a collective. The events of 2020 have shown us that whenever we are in the false sense of security of 'old habits', life will surprise us. Building and nurturing the muscle of courage will mean we will be able to flex around the unforeseen.

Summary:

Our performance relies on our ability to manage our emotions safely regardless of our environment or it's challenges

Our collective performance relies on our ability to create mindsafety

Consciousness (self and other), compassion (self and towards others) and courageous behaviours are our tools for high performance teaming

Questions:

1. This week I have been feeling in control of my emotions
2. This week I have noticed myself keeping silent about things I think
3. This week I have felt safe at work
4. This week we have been working well as a team
5. Our achievements this week have been remarkable

About the Author:

Dr Amy Silver

Amy is a psychologist, speaker and author on the management of emotions for high performance at work. Her programs teach people to have more courageous communication for remarkable outcomes. Amy runs powerful high performance teaming programs. She teaches people how to stand up, speak up, control anger and anxiety, change and innovate, driving psychologically safe teams maximising collective intelligence.

Amy has a Doctorate in Clinical Psychology, Masters in Forensic Psychiatry, Masters in Performance, Bachelor with Honours in Psychology and further therapeutic training in cognitive therapies such as Cognitive Analytic Therapy, Compassion Therapy, and Acceptance & Commitment Therapy. She has published widely in academic journals and more accessible magazines and now publishes fortnightly in a popular business-focused blog/vlog called *Silverlinings.* She is a contributing author in many books including the acclaimed *Oxford Handbook of Behavioural Experiments (for Oxford University)* and *Unite (ed. Julia Steel).* She is the author of the books *Conversations Create Growth* and *Brace for Impact (both available on her website)* and *The Loudest Guest: How to control your fear,* to be published February 2021 and available through all bookshops and online.

CHAPTER FIFTEEN

Tilt

Callum McKirdy

Bell curves rule the world. The concept of standardisation is omnipresent in Western society to the point we have created entire systems based on the bell curve. Think education with standardised testing, government funding measures based on socio-economic factors, political party size as left and right of 'centre'. The economy, internet and manufacturing have all been developed with those in the curve's hump front of mind.

In our organisations, we recruit for fit, based on criteria describing an ideal candidate. Both performance and pay is reviewed against criteria according to a scale devised with an average. The long-standing employee engagement survey delivers a bell-curve of results; the HR and leadership response to which seeks to move the central beer-belly of the curve to the right; a mammoth task that more often than not fails to deliver on expectations .... expectations that are once again based on a bell-curve approach.

During the COVID-19 pandemic, entire nations took up the fight to flatten the curve focusing on the middle as the area of most importance. *"Bring down the middle"* they said, and take pressure off the health system, and they were correct. This reference once again brought the mighty bell-curve into our homes, communities, and businesses.

Indeed, the common bell curve is otherwise known as a 'normal' distribution curve. It is our obsession with and struggle to remain in a state of normality that has seen our organisational systems and structures suffer greatly. The only way to respond to the pandemic was to temporarily abandon the system itself – to pack-up and go home. Production and manufacturing lines were shut down, entire towers of offices populated by most of the workforce were abandoned. Home became the workplace.

While we rejoiced in how promptly teams made the transition, productivity still dropped. We accepted this and quickly blamed the virus, internet speed and even the distraction of our own children. Yet, it was our bell curve obsession that left many organisations cumbersome, inflexible, and fragile in early 2020.

Management systems have barely changed in fifty years. We recruit for fit – fit determined by bell curve analysis and groupthink about what ideal looks like from a familiarity perspective. From a sea of difference, we select sameness for comfort around *'people like me'* for ease of managing because we get how these people think and can predict how they will likely behave. Our unconscious bias for minds like mine means we make only token attempts to seek out different perspectives, which only serve to reinforce the status quo.

An opportunity to think differently about different thinking

Winston Churchill and most recently Chicago Mayor Rahm Emanuel have been quoted as having said:

> “*Never let a good crisis go to waste!*”

Being forced to work somewhere else away from our workmates afforded a golden opportunity to make new connections and gain valuable insights about who and how we work. We were able to see our teams differently, to see the individuals in their own homes and invite them into ours. We got to try new ways of working, and crucially, to look at old work processes, behaviours and habits and question not only why we do these, but also:

- Do they even make sense?
- How do they inhibit and stifle growth and performance? and
- What might better and different use of natural talent look like?

All this points to an overarching opportunity for greater appreciation of difference and the innate power of diversity. Critically, we now have an opportunity to think differently together and get used to how that feels; something we have shied away from up until now.

As the world was put on hold - told to down tools, go home and stay there - perhaps we should look to never pick up many of those same tools again but instead choose another implement. Perhaps, if we do pick up the same tools, let us consider whether we were wielding them correctly. Those old tools – processes, practices, ways of thinking and working, meeting and communicating, managing and leading – served a purpose designed by the influential minds among the masses, with the masses in mind. Perhaps it is time to make better use of that tool and harness the collective and individual power of the mind itself.

When we think about diversity in organisations, we often think about things that are visible - gender and ethnicity, for example. Often, we can see these types of diversity just by looking around at the faces in a room. But this misses some critical elements of diversity. Behind every one of our differently coloured, shaped, cleansed, toned and moisturised faces, we all have a brain. Most are wired the same way; a few are wired quite differently. Known as Neurodiverse, this term refers to recognising and respecting neurological differences of a minority among our workforces — including autism, attention deficit hyperactivity disorder and dyslexia - the same way we do other differences. As such, a 'diversity' perspective that considers variation is the only logical approach – an approach that transcends almost all other categories used in diversity and inclusion initiatives.

Like an umbrella, neurodiversity sits across gender, race and orientation. It is a "no-brainer" to make better use of this hidden potential. Further, it is from the edges of the bell curve that innovation has occurred. We simply assumed the leaders of innovation have been rare geniuses – and they have been. Yet, many more of these genius minds lay hidden among our workforces because where you have a difference, you have an ability to make a difference.

Where you have difference, you have an ability to make a difference.

Harnessing untapped genius

While naturally occurring, being few in number and not fitting the norm, means neurodiverse people reside at the edge of the bell curve. Viewed as outliers and surrounded by stigma and fear, neurodiverse brains are widely misunderstood. Growing up in a world not designed with them in mind, neurodiverse people are not only last picked for the playground sports team, they are often inadvertently excluded from entry into our organisations. Those that do make it through the selection process often experience fear and a need to hide their true selves. Some are labelled problem children by managers afraid of facilitating conversations that explore divergent thinking. For many neurodiverse employees, the frustration of being merely observed and never truly seen means work is more a prison that constrains their potential for immense positive impact, rather than a prism through which the spectrum of their talents can be displayed.

The COVID-19 pandemic has exposed a need to do things differently. Within every workplace's cohort of differently wired thinkers lies a powerful potential to not just reclaim organisational success but surpass it in leaps and bounds. Neurodiverse employees not only think differently, they have had to develop ingenious workarounds and ways of living in a world not set up for them. What's more, they can possess extraordinary abilities to:

- hyper-focus for long periods in deep analysis
- display uninhibited creativity and problem solving
- connect seemingly disparate idea threads, and
- empathise deeply enabling early rapport and high trust

In the years leading up to the COVID crisis very few organisations purposefully sought to leverage the power of neurodiverse employees.

In fact, the vast majority of D&I strategies make no mention of targeting neurodiverse members of society or indeed existing employees – a travesty given they already exist in our businesses. We simply fail to recognise them as assets and it's time we changed this.

The imperative of reimagining the workplace

The fact we call our workplaces organisations suggests they're ordered, arranged and organised by a set of criteria – criteria designed to find a place for everyone so long as you are yourself designed in a shape that 'fits' our mould.

Maybe the future requires organisations to be less 'organised' in a rigid sense and instead be flexible in thinking, design and support?

Indeed, it's the organisations who take the time right now to think differently about different thinking and move to capitalise on the opportunity hiding in plain sight that will thrive over the coming months and years. Specifically, this requires:

1. Audacious leaders unafraid to hire, uncover and lead diverse teams;
2. Empathic people management systems and practices designed to unlock and enable the power of difference across the workplace; and
3. A culture of curiosity that celebrates rebel ideas and the unleashing of natural talents.

We should seek out the outliers, the diverse and different challengers, the problem children, the introverts and extroverts alike and empower them throughout their entire journey as your employee.

From a practical perspective this means reviewing the systems used to manage and lead people, and assess if they fully enable or disable neurodiverse people, such as your:

- Attraction & Brand strategies – do you target the natural tendencies and places people with specific skills and traits congregate?
- Recruitment & Selection tools and approaches – do these closely match the work tasks, situations and environment staff will face? Do they seek diversity or simply narrow the pool of candidates?
- On-Boarding processes – are these generic or tailored to the wants, needs and desires of each individual?
- Environment – what reasonable accommodations are you willing to provide to maximise the potential of individual employees?
- Leadership development – do you provide training and support for leaders to have empathy for and an ability to deal with the occasional challenges neurodiverse staff bring?
- Development & Performance Improvement options – are teams developed in ways that harness their individual and collective uniqueness?
- Rewards & Recognition policies – do you discuss with staff how they want their contribution recognised?

A future of unleashed neurodiversity

Transforming your workplace into a safe haven of trading ideas and facilitating interesting conversations by actively embracing both diversity of thought and thinking, is the new imperative. To do this we must rethink our people management systems, processes and paradigms, which currently nurture the status quo and inadvertently stifle different thinkers. For generations we have excluded a demographic that could well be our answer to the very barriers we face coming out of this new era of societal and economic disruption.

Fixed thinking has led to unconscious bias serving an agenda, just not the agenda workplaces now require. We need to reimagine the agenda of work – to think differently about delivered value and to lead neurodiverse people in ways that speak to and engage them to add the value that comes naturally to them; to find a true balance between the value people add and that which organisations add to their people.

From a performance standpoint, perhaps it is time we overtly elevate difference and utilise people in shorter, more specific sprints rather than have them labour and hang on trying to add value in areas they no longer suit. Doing so will see internal networks of ideas, beliefs, perspectives and strategies become more diverse in thought and produce decisions considered from all angles that best suit your context. Your own individual and collective abilities to challenge, question and critique can grow as your people discuss ideas not individuals; potential not politics; progress not power-play.

At the very least, it is time leaders considered how they can uncover, unlock and unleash the potential that exists in the hidden diversity across their organisation.

Summary:

Most organisations and their cultures have been built on assumptions developed for the masses by those who reside in the middle of the bell curve. This inadvertently hinders success and often actively excludes diversity of thought and thinking by reinforcing groupthink and the status quo. It leaves many businesses unprepared for mass disruption.

The COVID crisis provides an opportunity to flip the paradigm of inclusion, diversity and belonging. It has long been argued performance can be lifted via greater visible diversity, yet we have achieved little. By zooming-out another layer and applying the umbrella perspective of harnessing neurodiversity through taking a good hard look at the processes used to recruit, engage, and retain neurodiverse staff, organisations can make substantial shifts in how they perform as they rebound in 2020 and beyond.

By making the decision now to lead an organisation prepared to think differently about different thinking, you can be a first mover in your industry and get the jump on your competition.

Questions:

1. How well do your HR and people management systems and practices consider diversity of thinking?
2. What does your culture really say about how difference is accepted, leveraged and amplified?
3. If you re-imagined your organisation from the ground-up today, where does your imagination begin and end? Do you know who in your organisation can extend that thinking?
4. What about your leadership style demonstrates you are unafraid to lead a fully diverse team?
5. If COVID-21 were to hit, what three things about your organisation would you wish you had thought differently about today?

About the Author:

Callum McKirdy

Callum McKirdy is a speaker, author, mentor and facilitator specialising in helping people think and behave differently in the workplace. With a successful 20 year career assisting leaders and teams across Australasia to develop radically authentic workplaces, Callum works with service-based organisations to make the most of their uniqueness.

His lived experience of neurodiversity and deep professional expertise in HR makes him an expert in bringing out the different perspectives people have but hold back at work; perfectly positioning him to assist teams, leaders and entire organisations transform their cultures into inclusive places where everyone is empowered and enabled to show-up as their best, true selves.

Callum speaks at industry conferences, facilitates high-impact creative workshops, trains teams, and mentors leaders daring enough to reimagine their organisation and create radically authentic workplaces.

www.callummckirdy.com

Return to the Perfect World

The hero returns back to her normal world.
Even if it hasn't changed, she has...

CHAPTER SIXTEEN

Engage

Mary Butler

The COVID-19 global pandemic had just been declared. On 13th March 2020 experts gathered at the headquarters of the World Health Organisation in Geneva, Switzerland, to deliver their regular press conference on COVID-19[1].

The panel of speakers included the President and CEO of the United Nations Foundation, the VP of global health from the UNF, the President of the Swiss Philanthropy Foundation and Dr Michael Ryan, Executive Director of the WHO Health Emergencies Programme.

1 World Health Organisation. COVID-19 Update, 2020. Transcript available at https://www.rev.com/blog/transcripts/world-health-organization-covid-19-update-march-13-2020.

Watching this panel media update, I was gripped by the composure and clarity of the team, in particular Dr Ryan. As he spoke, I grabbed a pen to capture the brilliance of his contribution and advice. I was intrigued by how this related to my experience working with leaders in the start-up and scale-up industry.

Dr Ryan shared lessons he'd learned from his work with the Ebola crisis. He wasn't dictating actions. He was providing clear guidance based on his experience and capability. He spoke of how countries need to address the challenges of facing this pandemic.

What really struck me was the language he used about how to lead in a crisis. *(Like me, Dr Ryan is Irish, so his accent caught my attention. #proud)* I have worked in the development of leaders for over 25 years globally, and I have never heard leadership capabilities described as succinctly as I did in this update.

Dr Ryan was using language we all know and understand. There was nothing particularly new in what he was saying. What was unusual though, was how specific the language was in addressing the exact challenges people were facing. It wasn't vague or generic. We weren't left wondering, or interpreting his message. It was clear, concise, and consistent.

Leaders are continually faced with change and new challenges. How they react or respond to them, particularly in the early stages, has massive implications for their business. The guidance shared by Dr Ryan at that event is pertinent to any leader facing change.

Ambiguity has required us to dig deep into our reserves

For leaders, the spread of COVID-19 meant new ways of working, flexibility like we've never known, lockdown, lack of visibility, hidden strengths, strange personalities, incessant baking, uncertainty, selfies, loss, grief, inconsistencies, panic buying, new expectations, fear, failure, compassion, survival, anxiety. We had no idea what to do. It hit us fast and it hit us hard.

A large-scale study of executives by Korn Ferry found *"90% of the problems [executives] face are ambiguous. With greater responsibility comes more ambiguity."*[2]. In a time of even greater uncertainty than ever, we started asking: 'Who can I lean on? Who can tell me what I should be doing? Who can I trust?'

The start-up industry is, by its very nature, an ambiguous one. One reason I enjoy working here is that people drawn to working in this environment are typically not risk-averse. They are used to curveballs and unexpected disappointments. They thrive on the unknown and the unexpected. Despite their natural comfort with uncertainty, this sudden change in how they work affected these leaders in the same way, and to a similar extent, as those in other industries. Generally, it's the start-ups choosing to disrupt, not to be disrupted.

Recent ambiguity has required us to dig deep into our reserves and draw on everything we know from our life experiences to find the

---

2 Burnison, G., 2020. 'Are We There Yet?'. Korn Ferry, [online] Available at: <https://www.kornferry.com/insights/articles/four-ways-getting-through-coronavirus-leadership>.

best way through. It has made us question our abilities, and has been a confronting exercise in reflection.

The pandemic has changed how we lead, forever. Any assumptions of the status quo need to be thrown out, accepting the new assumption that nothing is certain. The leadership skills and capabilities that worked until now will not be enough for us to continue to survive.

We used to say leadership capability must focus on cost-cutting and efficiency. More recently, the focus for leaders has been on agility, resilience and adaptability. Today, we need leaders to be all of those things, but with an additional emphasis on being kind and compassionate.

We need to demonstrate empathy and strength, to not delay in making tough decisions and to be clear in our direction. We must be consistent in our engagement with our teams and the business. To help our teams move forward, as leaders we need to be, as a recent Forbes article calls it - 'ambiguity absorbers'[3]; providing clear, albeit changeable, direction to our team despite the inherent uncertainty we find ourselves in.

No one has escaped this crisis. Everyone has been impacted. It happened fast, and without warning. Those leaders who had the strength and ability to adapt quickly have had the most positive impact.

---

3 Duncan, R., 2020. Want To Lead In A Crisis? Be An Ambiguity Absorber. Forbes, [online] Available at: <https://www.forbes.com/sites/rodgerdeanduncan/2020/04/09/want-to-lead-in-a-crisis-be-an-ambiguity-absorber/#3b7d78e31063>.

Like many significant events, tragic as they may be, COVID-19 hasn't been all bad news for business. *"Telehealth, edtech, cybersecurity and e-commerce sectors have recorded significant growth and attracted investment during this time." "It's not about going back to the way we did things pre-COVID. It's also not about doing things the way we have done it during the crisis. It's about reimagining each of these markets.* [4]*"* says Paul Bassat, co-founder of Square Peg Venture Capital, and jobs giant Seek.

Dr Ryan's media updated addressed the following four key lessons from the Ebola crisis that can be applied to leadership in any situation.

1. Paralysis is a natural but destructive response to ambiguity

Paralysis caused by our fear of failure can have a crippling effect on leadership. It can manifest in so many destructive ways - indecision, procrastination, distrust, avoidance. People need visible and consistent leadership. They need to know what's expected of them, in particular in times of uncertainty.

This paralysis snowballs into our teams. As leaders, we need to ensure that our teams are comfortable taking risks, knowing that they may not always get things right. As Zoë Routh advises in her book 'Composure', we need to 'destigmatise failure' - *"If the team members associate failure with disapproval, or worse... then the focus becomes risk-avoidance and covering up errors."*[5]

---

4 Palmer-Derrien, S., 2020. "Era of innovation": Square Peg surpasses $1 billion in funding assets as Paul Bassat predicts post-pandemic tech boom. SmartCompany, [online] Available at: <https://www.smartcompany.com.au/startupsmart/news/square-peg-1-billion-paul-bassat-covid-19/>.

5 Routh, Z., 2015. Composure: How Centred Leaders Make The Biggest Impact. 1st ed. Inner Compass Australia.

Fear of failure is often caused by self-doubt. This impacts our teams by intensifying their doubt – doubt in our capabilities as leaders, and doubt in their ability to perform as a cohesive team. In the Trillion Dollar Coach, Bill Campbell is credited with the phrase *"You can't afford to doubt. You need to commit. You can make mistakes, but you can't have one foot in and one foot out, because if you aren't fully committed then the people around you won't be either. If you're in, be in."*[6]

We need to allow ourselves to make mistakes and not let self-doubt drive our paralysis. Self-doubt is difficult to overcome. In many ways it makes no sense. We know this academically, but our mindset needs to shift to be able to recognise it and take action to beat it.

2. Leave no one behind

What struck me the most with Dr Ryan was the empathy and compassion he showed for those who are more vulnerable. *"When we speak about that vulnerability, we cannot forget migrants. We cannot forget undocumented workers. We cannot forget prisoners in prisons. They may be serving a sentence, but they deserve no less protection under the law than others."* [7]

When building teams, how often do we stigmatise and exclude people we consider less capable *(i.e. less like us!)*? We select the 'best' people we can. But what does the best mean? It's not the smartest, or the most experienced, or the most senior.

6 Schmidt, E., Rosenberg, J. and Eagle, A., 2019. Trillion Dollar Coach: The Leadership Playbook Of Silicon Valley's Bill Campbell. London: John Murray.

7 Op. cit, World Health Organisation, 2020

I recall working for an organisation early in my career where there was a restructure of the functions. I was initially excited to be working with a senior leader, Hugh, who I really admired. This feeling was quickly replaced with dismay. He had created a new team that seemed to be a broad mix of capability, personality, and experience. In ways it felt like Hugh had selected a team of misfits *(the vulnerable?)* left over from the restructure. I was quite miffed, to be honest!

I was wrong, very wrong. Yes, we were a mixed bag, but what I came to realise was that Hugh's strength was in recognising the value of each individual's potential in a diverse team. The synergy created by this team was incredibly effective. Creativity, innovation, and teamwork thrived.

During lockdown, people have responded very differently to working differently. Many people have had additional responsibilities placed on them, affecting their work. For many, their home situation has required an interesting shift - we've all seen those videos of children climbing on their parents during meetings, cats walking across laptops, and a few unfortunately placed cameras! There have been challenges of home education, fear for elderly parents, friends and neighbours truly isolated in isolation. It has been easy for people to get left behind.

We have learned to be more compassionate. But it took a while. In the early days, leaders' expectations of their teams were the same as though everyone was still working under normal conditions.

Over time, we all started to recognise the shift that was happening. People were being kinder to one another, more accepting and accommodating. With so much uncertainty still ahead of us, it's important we continue to ensure nobody gets left behind.

"When we get to the other side of this pandemic, my hope is that more of us learn to lead inclusively and with empathy, not only in crisis but also in calm."[8]

Leave no one behind.

3. A coordinated approach to crisis is essential

Leaders now understand the importance of being prepared for the unexpected and anticipating challenges. Leaders who have been most successful know how to mobilise their teams quickly, prioritise their actions, and tackle the challenges as a coordinated team.

Leaders in crisis actively involve the right stakeholders. They include people from across the board. There is no special allowance for hierarchy. They think: 'who else needs to know?'. Nobody likes surprises. Communication and inclusion are particularly critical at a time that's full of surprise.

A number of years ago I worked for an incredible HR Director, Kate. When I was hired into the role, I wanted to make sure I communicated with her in a way that was most effective. I asked her what was most important to her in keeping her across what work was being done, and what was still on the list. I was expecting her to say 'weekly meetings, with regular email updates', as I had

8 Tulshyan, R., 2020. How to Be an Inclusive Leader Through a Crisis. Harvard Business Review, [online] Available at: <https://hbr.org/2020/04/how-to-be-an-inclusive-leader-through-a-crisis>.

experienced with previous leaders. I loved Kate's response and it's one I have carried through my own career as a leader. The one thing Kate expected from her team was - no surprises. She explained that if she didn't know the good and the bad of what was going on, it would look bad for our whole team, and more importantly, she couldn't have our backs.

For Kate to lead effectively, she wasn't particularly interested in hearing the minutiae of our daily activities. She trusted us to manage that. She needed to never be blindsided, even if it was bad news, because that's the only way she could manage the issue coherently. By asking us 'who else needs to know', the benefit to this open approach was twofold. It allowed us as her team to be vulnerable and share our mistakes, in a safe environment, without risk of reprimand. It also ensured that Kate was always in a position to engage the right stakeholders by just asking 'who else needs to know?'.

Keeping people coordinated through COVID has been difficult. Working from home became the norm. Flexible working took on a new meaning and leaders had to work harder to stay connected with their teams. It challenged our limits of trust.

Trust will continue to be tested on a new level. It's not always about high level trust. In her book Dare to Lead, Brene Brown says 'trust is earned in the smallest moments'[9]

Leaders have had to work harder on helping people feel trusted and:

- Engaged - listened to
- Enabled – have the tools to do their job

9 Brown, B., n.d. Dare To Lead. London: Vermillion.

- Empowered – have no unnecessary restrictions
- Educated – have the information they need
- Encouraged – feel supported and motivated
- Emotionally connected – they see the impacts of their efforts

Atlassian is an Australian software multinational with 4,000 Atlassians across seven global offices, whose co-founders vaulted to the top of the 2019 BRW Young Rich List with a combined wealth of $26.7bn. Their leaders have been working hard to engage all team members, consistently. *"Since the crisis began (our approach) is to invite our staff into conversation with HR and the executive team, and it's working. We're able to get a holistic picture of what our people need, address those needs, and gather feedback—then rinse, repeat, rinse, repeat."*[10]

4. Speed trumps perfection.

In her book, 'Ish'[11], Lynne Cazaly writes *"it's time to let go of those expectations of perfection on our first attempt. Rather than perfection, go for iteration."* Dr Ryan shares this as 'speed trumps perfection'. Moving quickly, with no regrets.

Earlier, I wrote about the internal conflict of paralysis, fear of failure and self-doubt causing us to delay in getting things done.

---

10 Rosen, T., 2020. This is the way to create an effective crisis response strategy. FastCompany, [online] Available at: <https://www.fastcompany.com/90513649/this-is-the-way-to-create-an-effective-crisis-response-strategy>.

11 Cazaly, L., 2019. Ish: The Problem With Our Pursuit For Perfection And The Life-Changing Practise Of Good Enough. 5th ed. Melbourne.

Speed trumps perfection also considers the external considerations of moving forward. It's about taking action before all of the information is available and drawing on what we know to be the likely path to help us make some tough decisions. *"One of the most difficult parts of making a choice about which opportunities to pursue is killing off other opportunities – it's much less daunting to 'keep our options open'."*[12] If we want clarity in an uncertain environment, we must favour action over analysis, progress over perfection, confidence over certainty, and a good choice over the perfect choice that never reveals itself.

The world watched as New Zealand Prime Minister, Jacinda Ardern, showed us how speed trumps perfection. She didn't wait for all of the information, or evidence of 'flattening the curve' in other countries. Instead, Jacinda demonstrated strong leadership by calling the shots early; giving clear direction; delivering consistent messaging; showing vulnerability; making herself available to the New Zealand people; not wavering in her convictions; listening to the right people; and making the tough decisions, quickly. Importantly, she did all this with empathy and compassion.

Latent Leaders

Overcoming paralysis and fear of failure; removing stigma and exclusion, leading with compassion; driving a coordinated approach; and moving quickly. These are leadership capabilities shared by Dr Ryan, and as demonstrated by leaders all over the world during the COVID-19 crisis.

There have been so many heroes of this pandemic. None of them have done it for notoriety, or for the promise of a promotion. These people are true leaders. Through compassion and care, action before

12 Hagan, A., 2019. Thriving In Complexity: The Art & Science Of Discovering Opportunity In The New Normal. 1st ed. Melbourne: Kienco.

information, with so much unknown, they did what they had to do, often at immense risk to themselves. How many of us as leaders need to put our fears, our hopes and our dreams aside just to do our jobs, without an expectation of reward? These heroes did this, for us.

What makes these people as leaders so effective isn't that they seek glory or kudos. Rather, at a time of ambiguity, they work to bring people together quickly to deliver a cohesive response. As Dr Ryan advises - don't be afraid of making mistakes, leave no one behind, engage deeply and move quickly.

Would you run a marathon if you couldn't tell anyone about it? A true leader does, every day.

Summary:

We need to lead differently. The leadership skills and capabilities that worked until now will not be enough for us to continue to survive.

We should learn from, and leverage, the lessons of past experiences.

Don't be afraid of making mistakes, leave no one behind, engage deeply and move quickly.

Questions:

1. As a leader, what past experiences can you leverage to help you respond to crisis?
2. How do you face ambiguity? How does this impact you and your team?
3. Are you paralysed by self-doubt and fear of failure? What can you do now to overcome this?
4. Are you conscious of inclusion? Do you engage all the right people, deeply? Do you leave no one behind?
5. Can you move quickly? Do you strive for perfection before action?

About the Author:

Mary Butler

Mary Butler designs, executes and delivers people strategy, working with Venture Capitalists, start-ups and scale-ups primarily in the tech sector. She works with senior leaders to build leadership and organisational capability, to help them to scale. She particularly enjoys working with people and organisations in transition.

With BSc and MBA qualifications, Mary has worked across a broad range of industries, across the globe. She has 25 years' experience in senior leadership roles in Talent Management and is the recipient of a number of global awards for excellence and innovation, including her role in delivering the world's first online masters in Cloud Computing.

Mary is the author of two books *"Recreate your career story: how to get clear on your career" (2019)* and *"Scalable People: who they are and why your business needs them" (2020).*

www.marybutler.net

CHAPTER SEVENTEEN

Sustain

Simon Rudderham

"*Now there's something you don't see everyday...*" I murmured as a lady in her late 40s passed by the window. Dressed in a matching shiny silver parachute material tracksuit and sporting a plastic face shield, she looked like what I'd imagine a henchperson from the Bond film Moonraker would look like if they tried to break a velodrome cycling record.

It was late March, and COVID-19 panic buying was in full swing. While many of my friends had ceased commuting into work and had set up their home office, I was unable to do so. Partly because as a retailer, my driveway would be too steep for a large number of my clients, but mainly because as a retail pharmacist, the constabulary don't tend to look too kindly on people selling drugs out of their garage.

She entered the front doors, prescription in hand, following the arrows on the ground for social distancing. She greeted a staff member at the register who politely asked some screening questions, and was then asked to sanitise her hands using the sanitiser provided. *"Of course!"* she said, and proceeded to put her prescriptions in her mouth while she sanitised her hands vigorously, then attempted to hand the prescriptions to a staff member.

facepalm

One of the key tenets of retail is having well trained staff who know their procedures. A slightly more nuanced rule is well trained customers who follow clues and tacit instructions to allow a processed flow thus assisting operations. But since COVID has thrown that out the window, what the hell do we do now?

Working from home was not really an option for me as a retail pharmacist. The constabulary don't tend to look too kindly on people selling drugs out of their garage.

Redesigning the retail environment

Pharmacy as a retail construct has undertaken considerable change. In decades gone by, the pharmacist was in an elevated position, his castle if you will, able to survey all that he had leased. This caused a problem, as the general public's accessibility to the pharmacist was restricted.

The newer retail pharmacy concepts have pharmacists not only on the same level as the loyal subjects, but also in an accessible manner. This forward pharmacy concept allows the client to converse with the pharmacist during the dispensing of the prescription, or able to approach for information, queries or treatment advice. This accessibility has allowed pharmacists to build a rapport with their customers. With the advent of COVID, this accessibility is now restricted. Sheets of plexiglass are being placed on prescription counters to protect staff and customers alike *(albeit whilst giving a point of view of what the salad bar at Sizzler used to see from behind the sneeze-guard)*, and it is difficult to build rapport through plexiglass.

Prior to COVID, barriers in retail were more associated with transactional interactions and staff security. Examples of this include a bank teller, a ticket salesperson at a theatre or a sports venue, or a console operator in a petrol station or 7-Eleven. In each of these examples, it could be argued that the primary role of the service operator is the exchange of goods for payment, with some advice functions possibly on offer. In retail pharmacy, the service offering is usually done in two separate steps: the advice and the transactions. The presence of the plexiglass can confuse the patient when presenting to the service section, with some trying to pay at the point of advice, or hovering to try to speak to the pharmacist not realising that spatially distanced line in front of the plexiglass counter is not the payment line, but instead the service line that they require.

All of these factors impede workflow and provide logistical issues for operations to overcome. A confused customer is usually an unhappy customer, and the onus is on the retail team to ensure that the new post-COVID layout is clearly designed, well-marked and as painless as possible for the incoming customer to follow.

COVID and the triple bottom line

The triple bottom line *(TBL)* is a framework developed by Elkington in 1994 that posits that companies focus as much on social and environmental concerns as they do on profit, thus achieving greater sustainability. Put simply, for an organisation to be sustainable, it must focus on people, profit and the planet. TBL theory holds that if an organisation solely looks at profits and ignores people and the planet, it cannot account for the full cost of doing business.

For larger organisations, there is often board involvement to safeguard company exposure to unethical practices and to keep management in check. In small to medium enterprises *(SMEs)* however, decision makers may be a sole trader, or a small conglomerate of managers, without the same degree of public and shareholder accountability.

In the post-COVID retail apocalypse of March, the new currency was toilet paper. While most retailers struggled to maintain regular supply to the stores due to unprecedented demand, sensible limits were set to ensure that there would be sufficient and timely access for all those who needed it. Meanwhile, Facebook Marketplace and Gumtree had bog roll offerings of six packs for $50. My business partner, while attempting to purchase toilet rolls through the wholesaler, mistakenly purchased 48 units of Viva paper towel. Realising the mistake before the delivery arrived, he organised a return authority, only to watch on in disbelief as the delivery driver attracted an orderly mob as he was making his delivery, like some sort of pied piper of poo-tickets. A very helpful member of the public already had a Stanley knife at the ready to open the outer slab and help himself to five packets of the towel, before distributing the remainder to the ever-growing members of the general public. Explanations that the paper products were designed for hand wiping were met with a glazed silence, so he shrugged, set a 2 packet per person maximum limit and sold 48 units of paper towel in 8 minutes.

The COVID situation has led to many such counterintuitive dilemmas for retailers. The *"stack em high, watch em fly"* approach has had to be re-evaluated as no longer good for long term business. While there is an opportunity to make a quick buck, there is a need to ensure that you are able to maintain supply for those who have a genuine need. Selling your inventory to the first available buyer is likely to be frowned upon by others in the community, who may be less likely to utilise your services in future: it is unsustainable as it puts profits above the community as a whole.

In retail, use of space is paramount. From an operations perspective, you would ideally like your clientele to traverse the entirety of your retail offering. This is far from a new concept. The placement of eggs, bread and milk at the back of supermarkets and the position of the register in a petrol station are designed to have the customer see as many impulse purchase lines as possible before paying. COVID-19 has changed the retail layout in many pharmacies however. Where multiple exits and entrances have been present in some stores, clients are now funnelled through the one entrance to ensure hand sanitisation and concierge questioning. Sections of the retail offering have been roped off from self-service.

While in 1994 Elkington was describing the planet's role in TBL, I'm not sure that slowing a pandemic was necessarily front of mind. In the COVID case, the role for SMEs to play has never been bigger. Actively denying access to sales in some key pharmacy retail sections is likely to be reducing the spread. Access to cosmetics, testers, reading glasses, sunglasses and giftware has been restricted to reduce the contact and likelihood of transmission. It is counterintuitive in retail to limit the number of clients who walk through your doors, yet COVID has forced maximum limits to ensure spatial and social distancing. All of these things fit into Elkington's TBL supposition, as failure to control virus spread risk is unsustainable. Too many people doing the wrong thing can lead to the shutting down of retail spaces, to the detriment of all and the benefit of none, including retailers themselves.

Resistance to change

Not sure if anyone has noticed, but COVID has changed the way in which we do things. I'm frequently observing the slightly nuanced changes, such as complete lockdown, limited numbers in retail spaces, frequent hand washing and the anxiety immediately prior to any announcement by the Premier or Prime Minister.

For many, change can be a pain in the butt if not explained properly, or there is a refusal to accept the reasons for the change. I'd like to say that in my retail experience, it tends to be the older clientele who struggle with change, but then I remember how irrationally irritated I get when supermarkets move things arounds *(THE MUSTARD WAS RIGHT HERE YESTERDAY!)*. Some adapt to change easily, others may struggle, and the need for change may need to be reinforced.

Hiatt's model of Resistance to Change *(2006)* suggests using an ADKAR method *(Awareness of the need to change, Desire to support and participate in the change, Knowledge of how to change, Ability to implement the required skills and behaviours and Reinforcement to sustain the change)*. At this stage, most of us are sitting at the reinforcement stage: we know why we need to change, we want to stop the virus spread, we know what we must do and we have implemented the skills of handwashing and mask-wearing, and now we just have to remember to do all of these things. Thinking back to the lady at the beginning of the piece in her futuristic jumpsuit and faceguard, putting her prescription in her mouth before handing it to the retail staff, she just had a bit of trouble with the implementation phase.

Yet as retailers, we are still dealing with clients completely resistant to change, or unwilling to complete the reinforcement phase of Hiatt's theory.

It is a condition of entry into the pharmacy in which I work to sanitise one's hands using the hand sanitiser provided upon entry. And yet we are still in June having pushback from some clients, with reasoning such as *"I just did that before", "I'm so sick of this"* to *"(vague babble about 5G and Bill Gates)"*. In the unique position as both a retailer and a healthcare provider, I feel a responsibility to help reinforce the change by seeking these clients out and thanking them for washing their hands and listening to their reasons for not washing their hands. Those who have just washed their hands are particularly thanked for understanding the need to wash their hands again, as they have travelled through the shopping centre prior to the entry of the store, and the need to protect the vulnerable clients who don't have the luxury of not attending the pharmacy. Those who are sick of it all, are also genuinely thanked for continuing to persist with this new change that 2020 has brought upon us. The conspiracy theorists? I point out that my science background means that I disagree with them, and that my priority is the safety of all clients, and then a polite thanks for abiding by our policy of handwashing.

I suspect that as we weave in and out of COVID lockdowns, the resistance to change will ebb and flow. I am well aware that we will not win over all clients, but that we must stick to our guns in order to ensure the safety of all, even if it means my hands see more alcohol than my liver this year.

Summary:

COVID has changed the retail and healthcare landscapes, making it more challenging to build rapport with customers.

Triple Bottom Line proposes that we put people and the planet above short-term profits. Though the temptation for unscrupulous operators will be to maximise profits in the short-term, this can lead to poor outcomes for the community as a whole and the long-term viability of a business.

A critical step in any change program is reinforcing the change to ensure it is sustained and becomes the "new normal".

Questions:

1. What's your role in raising people's awareness of the news ways of working?
2. What are the new barriers you're experiencing that are driving the redesign of how we work?
3. What initiatives are you putting in place to address Triple Bottom Line requirements *(people, profit, planet)*?
4. What resistance to change are you observing and how are you addressing it?
5. In your business, how are you reinforcing the necessary changes to protect your people, your profit and our planet long-term?

About the Author:

Simon Rudderham

Simon Rudderham is a pharmacist, and has 13 years of leadership experience in the Pharmaceutical industry. Simon has well-developed business acumen with a commitment to adding value to organisations, and a proven history of developing and sustaining business growth. He has a keen interest in customer service, strategic operations and change management. Simon has a B.Pharm from the University of Sydney, and an MBA from the Australian Institute of Business.

LinkedIn: https://www.linkedin.com/in/simon-rudderham/

CPSIA information can be obtained
at www.ICGtesting.com
Printed in the USA
LVHW051558181020
669092LV00011B/1054

9 780648 966128